Hodder Cambridge Primary

English

Learner's Book
Stage 5

Anne Basden
Series Editor: Dr John Bennett

The Publishers would like to thank the following for permission to reproduce copyright material:

Acknowledgements

p4, from *www.nhs.uk/changeforlife*, accessed July 2014; p10; from *www.teenshealth.org*, accessed July 2014; p14, from *www.eathappyproject.com,* accessed July 2014; p20, p23 from *Mufaro's Beautiful Daughters* by John Steptoe from *www.gaiaonline.com*, accessed July 2014; p26, 28, 29 from *Journey to Jo'burg* by Beverley Naidoo reproduced by permission of The Agency (London) Ltd © Beverley Naidoo, 1985, all rights reserved and enquiries to The Agency (London) Ltd, 14 Pottery Lane, London W11 4LZ; p31, p34, 36 from *Fly, Eagle, Fly!* by Christopher Gregorwski, text copyright © Christopher Gregorwski reprinted with the permission of Margaret K. McElderry Books, an imprint of Simon & Schuster Children's Publishing Division. Reproduced in Africa by permission of Niki Daly for a donation to the Red Cross Hospital Primary School, Cape Town, South Africa; p37, p40 from *Chocolate Cake* by Michael Rosen; p43, from *The Tale of Custard the Dragon* by Ogden Nash copyright © 1936 Ogden Nash, renewed. Reprinted by permission of Curtis Brown Ltd; p45, *Sun is Laughing* by Grace Nichols from *A is Amazing: Poems about Feelings*, reproduced with permission of Curtis Brown Group Ltd, London on behalf of Grace Nichols © Grace Nichols 1994; p56, p58, p60, p61 from *The Amazing Story of Adolphus Tips* by Michael Morpurgo reprinted in World (excl. US) by permission of HarperCollins Publishers Ltd and in US by permission of Scholastic Inc./Scholastic Press © (2005) Michael Morpurgo; p65, p66 from *The Brilliant World of Tom Gates* by Liz Pichon, published by Scholastic books; p66, p116, p125 by Anne Basden © Anne Basden 2014. p71, from *The Golden Touch of King Midas* by Paul Perro reproduced by permission of Stephen Dinning; p80, from *The Ballad of Robin Hood – Traditional* (author unknown); p82, p84, p85, p86, p87, p88, p89, p90 from *North Child* by Edith Pattou, text reproduced by permission of Usborne Publishing Ltd, 83-85 Saffron Hill, London, EC1N 8RT, UK, *www.usborne.com*, text copyright © 2003 Edith Pattou; p96, p100, p102, p104, p106, p107, p108, p110 from *Charlie and the Chocolate Factory – A Play* by Roald Dahl and Richard George, published by Penguin Books Ltd. and reproduced by permission of David Higham Associates; p97, p98, p101, p103, p105 from *Charlie and the Chocolate Factory* by Roald Dahl published by Penguin Books Ltd. and reproduced by permission of David Higham Associates; p132, p133 by Paul Cookson reproduced by permission of the author; p138, p143 by Gervase Phinn reproduced by permission of the author; p135, *Hurricane* by Dionne Brand from Earth Magic, poems by Dionne Brand and illustrations by Eugenie Fernandes, used by permission of Kids Can Press Ltd, Toronto, Canada, text © 1979, 2006 Dionne Brand; p136, p137 from *Alice's Adventures in Wonderland* by Lewis Carroll; p139, from *Mum'll Be Coming Home Today* by Michael Rosen © Michael Rosen.

Every effort has been made to trace all copyright holders, but if any have been inadvertently overlooked the Publishers will be pleased to make the necessary arrangements at the first opportunity.

Practice Test exam-style questions and sample answers are written by the author.

Although every effort has been made to ensure that website addresses are correct at time of going to press, Hodder Education cannot be held responsible for the content of any website mentioned in this book. It is sometimes possible to find a relocated web page by typing in the address of the home page for a website in the URL window of your browser.

Hachette UK's policy is to use papers that are natural, renewable and recyclable products and made from wood grown in sustainable forests. The logging and manufacturing processes are expected to conform to the environmental regulations of the country of origin.

Orders: please contact Hachette UK Distribution, Hely Hutchinson Centre, Milton Road, Didcot, Oxfordshire, OX11 7HH. Telephone: +44 (0)1235 827827. Email education@hachette.co.uk Lines are open from 9 a.m. to 5 p.m., Monday to Friday. You can also order through our website: www.hoddereducation.com

© Anne Basden 2015
First published in 2015 by
Hodder Education,
An Hachette UK Company
Carmelite House
50 Victoria Embankment
London EC4Y 0DZ

Impression number   13
Year   2021

Cover illustration by Sandy Lightley
Illustrations by Marleen Visser
Typeset in Swissforall in 12pt by Resolution
Printed by CPI Group (UK) Ltd, Croydon CR0 4YY

A catalogue record for this title is available from the British Library

ISBN 978 1471 830761

Contents

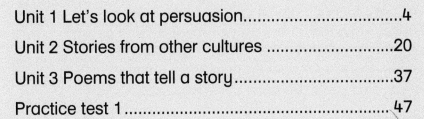

Unit 1 Let's look at persuasion

Eat Well – Stay Well – Look Well

You wouldn't eat sugar straight out of the packet, but do you think about the sugar hiding in the other things you eat and drink? The problem is that too much sugar can mean too much energy which can lead to extra fat being stored in the body. This carries all sorts of health risks!

You'll be amazed at how much sugar is hiding in food – even food that doesn't taste sweet. Try to swap food and drink with added sugar to healthier, sugar-free options which are much better for you.

Eating too much sugar can also affect your teeth and cause tooth decay, which is very unpleasant.

Many of us enjoy salt on our food. You might think you don't eat much salt as you don't add it to your food. What you don't know is that salt is hidden in everyday foods that don't even taste that salty – like bread, breakfast cereal and pizza! It means that most of us are eating much more salt than we think.

The bad news is that eating too much salt is not good for you.

Fruit and vegetables are a good source of vitamins, minerals and fibre which all help to keep you healthy. We all know that it is important for us to eat at least five portions of fruit and vegetables every day, but how many of us actually manage it?

Luckily, it can be easier than you think to get your 'FIVE A DAY'. The great thing is you don't have to make a big change to your diet or go without the foods you love.

Helpful hints

Persuasive texts try to convince us that the views the writer holds are the ones we should have too.

The key features of this text are:

- title – this should tell you what the writing is about
- opening statement – this should attract the reader's attention
- focus on the reader – it is your view that must be addressed.

1 Read the text about healthy eating on page 4 and then answer the following questions:
  a   What is the writer trying to persuade the reader to do?
  b   Which food is bad for your teeth?
  c   How does the writer give advice to the reader?
  d   Name two bad things that can happen if you eat too much sugar.
  e   Why is it difficult to check how much salt you have eaten?

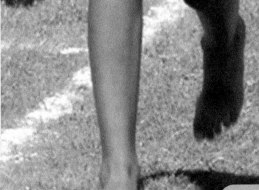

Helpful hints

Clauses always have a subject (who or what) and verb (a doing word).
There are two clauses in this sentence:
● <u>We need to eat healthy food</u> and <u>do lots of exercise</u>.
They have been joined by the word and.

2 Copy each sentence and underline the words which join the clauses.
  a   Fruit makes a good snack when you are hungry.
  b   Salt adds flavour to food but too much salt is not good for you.
  c   A good way to keep healthy is to play a sport or go to the gym.
  d   Remember to walk up the stairs instead of using the lift.
  e   We have learnt about salt and sugar in our diet, now we need to read about the fat in butter and ghee.

Key features

I can use apostrophes for shortened forms.

1 The text about healthy eating on page 4 is a **persuasive** text. Look at the list of key features below and write the two that are from persuasive texts:
- focus on the reader
- opening statement
- written in columns
- numbered steps.

2 Some words in the text have been shortened using an apostrophe. Copy and complete the table, writing the pair of words that each contraction stands for.

Contraction	Pair of words
wouldn't	
you'll	
doesn't	
don't	
it's	
I've	

Helpful hints

We use an **apostrophe** to show a letter or letters are missing in a word. This is called a **contraction** or an **apostrophe to show omission**. For example: Please **don't** run in the corridor. Don't is the shortened form of 'do not'.

3 Write your own persuasive text about a new play area you would like to have in your school. Think about where this could be placed and what it could include. Write it as a speech to read out to your class. Address your audience personally and use words and phrases to support your ideas and ask questions. Afterwards, check through your story and underline any words that are spelt incorrectly. Write these words in your spelling journal and practise spelling them correctly.

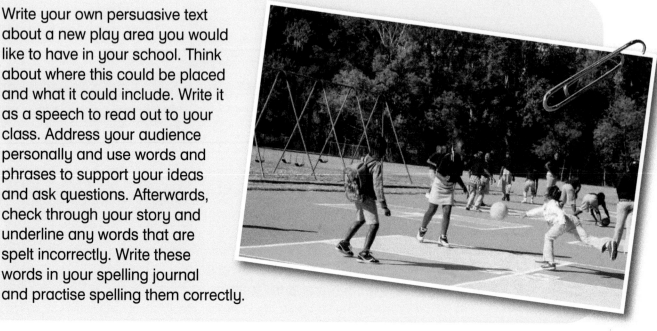

Answering questions about a text

I can identify features of persuasive texts.

I can answer questions about a text.

The World of Food

The world of food can be a confusing place, so in our farm store we are working to help children understand where their food comes from and how it is made.

Take your children out to explore where food comes from. It is not just outdoors, bringing them into our store will give them a chance to bake bread, fillet a fish and learn about different foods.

You can also follow a farm trail, meet the people who grow your food and learn how the food gets to your plate.

If you can't manage a trip to our store, we can come to visit you at school.

Talk Partners

Texts are written for an audience (someone who reads them). Look back at the Helpful hints box on page 4 to remind yourself of the features of persuasive texts. Talk about the following questions with your partner.

a Who is the text above written for?
b Who is this text written by?
c What is the purpose of this text?

1 Write a letter to a local food producer or large shop where some foods are produced on site. Explain that you would like to learn how they promote healthy eating and what products they have which support this. Think about the information you would like to receive from them.

Looking at plurals

1 Copy and complete this table to show the plurals of foods you can buy in a shop.

singular	plural
one loaf of bread	two _____ _____ _____
one potato	two _____
one cherry	two _____
one box of eggs	two _____ _____ _____
one pot of ghee	two _____ _____ _____

2 Add a subordinate clause to these main clauses:
a   I like to eat lunch outside _____.
b   The shop was closed _____.
c   Mum will take us to the park _____.

3 Write out the words from the boxes below to make a sentence. Remember to punctuate it properly.

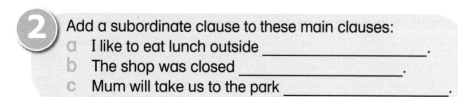

arrange a visit

who are in Stage 5

for all of the children

I am writing to

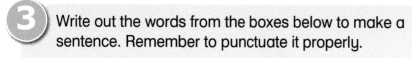

to learn more about healthy eating

Helpful hints

A **simple sentence** has one **main clause**. For example, 'The children always work hard'. A **complex sentence** is made when a **subordinate clause** is added. A subordinate clause provides more information but would not make sense on its own without the main clause.
For example: *The children always work hard* (**main clause**) *especially in science* (**subordinate clause**).

Helpful hints

The writer of the text on page 7 has used **alliteration**. This is when two or more words next to each other begin with the same letter. For example, *bake bread* and *fillet fish*. This gives the words more emphasis and can help the reader remember them more easily. Can you find two examples of alliteration in the text?

Talk Partners   With a partner read out loud the alliteration in the text then work together to make up some more which could help emphasise the things which are sold or activities which go on in large supermarkets. For example, buy breadfruit.

Active hobbies

I can find information in non-fiction texts.

I can present an argument to persuade others to adopt my point of view.

Top tips – get going your way!

Eating a healthy diet is only a part of living a healthy life style. Take up an active hobby too and you will soon feel on top of the world.

A walk in the park
Walking is a great active hobby that you can do on your own or with friends.

Run wild!
Running is a really fun way of burning energy. It can be with a group of friends, or on your own. Set your own pace and see if you can beat your own record.

Get on your bike!
Cycle around your local park or try an organised bike ride. Many of them are short distances and are a great way to meet new people.

Splash out!
Whether it's a regular splash with family or friends or swimming lengths, it's a fun way to get active.

1 The text above has sub-headings which help the reader to find information more quickly.
Identify which sub-heading would tell you about:
* swimming
* cycling
* running.

2 What activity do you do to keep fit? Think of a catchy heading and write about it. Your aim is to persuade a friend to join in with your chosen activity.

A personal story

Zach's story

I love great food – fresh, local food that doesn't travel for days before it gets to you. I've turned this interest into a healthy baking business that's expanded and grown. I use local fresh eggs, spelt flour, real butter. No preservatives. If I can't pronounce it I don't eat it!

I discovered a love for baking and cooking when I was 8 (I'm now 15).

I found out that I loved working in the kitchen. Soon I was making many of the meals and all of the baked goods for my family. Then I saw a notice that said a national health store chain was looking for local bakers. I filled in an application form and I was accepted. My dad delivers my products, my mum helps out and my two brothers help with packaging.

My belief on healthy eating is: 'Go local!' Eat fresh. Try new things.

Glossary

spelt flour: a nutty and slightly sweet flour used to make bread and pasta

preservatives: chemicals added to food to help it stay fresh

Speech

I can understand the difference between direct and reported speech.

Talk Partners

Zach wrote about how he set up a small business. You have an opportunity to ask him some questions. Work with a talk partner to interview Zach. Write the questions together then each take on a role – as Zach or the interviewer.

1 Write these examples of reported speech as direct speech:

a Zach believes that fresh, local food is best.

b Zach knows that healthy food does not need preservatives.

c Mum and Dad say that they are very proud of Zach's achievements.

d The customers that buy Zach's bread tell their friends it has a nutty taste.

2 Add the punctuation correctly into these examples of direct speech.

a It is my ambition to produce food which helps people lead a healthy lifestyle Zach explained. My family all support me.

b We all support Zach with his business said his parents. Even his brother helps with packaging.

Helpful hints

Direct speech is when someone is actually speaking. There are five rules for direct speech. For example:

"I was only eight years old when I started baking and cooking," said Zach.

1. The words spoken go **inside** the speech marks.

2. Every spoken sentence begins with a capital letter.

3. If you interrupt a spoken sentence with something about the speaker, you don't need a capital letter to begin the second part.

4. You must punctuate **before** closing the speech marks. This is often a comma, but could be a full stop, an exclamation mark or a question mark.

5. When the speaker changes, you start a new paragraph.

Reported speech is when you report what someone else has said. For example:

Zach said that he was eight years old when he started baking and cooking.

Fairtrade

A little of what you fancy does you good

- Chocolate helps your memory.
- Chocolate helps you feel good.
- Chocolate may prevent tooth decay.
- Chocolate helps you live longer.

Research shows that eating just a little chocolate can be good for you. Even better if that chocolate has been produced through FAIRTRADE.

FAIRTRADE is a simple yet incredibly important idea – it's all about making sure the people who produce the things you buy are paid fairly for their work. Buy something with a FAIRTRADE logo on it and you are making sure that the

people who worked to produce it are being paid a fair amount and have good working conditions.

There are lots of other things you can do. You can help your school to become a FAIRTRADE school – just ask your teacher to help and get involved.

Did you know?

Planning for the future

Money raised through FAIRTRADE is being used to build schools, provide clean water and start new FAIRTRADE schemes. Tate and Lyle (leading sugar manufacturers) use FAIRTRADE farmers to provide their cane sugar.

Pronouns and prefixes

I can use possessive pronouns.

I can use prefixes and suffixes.

1 Read the text on page 12. Write out these sentences using the correct possessive pronoun from the brackets.
a I would like to give (my/mine/me) opinion about chocolate.
b People must make up (their/they/theirs) own minds.
c FAIRTRADE is working so people can sell (their/they/theirs) products for a fair price.
d FAIRTRADE is helping (it/us/them) to support food producers.

2 Change the meaning of these words by adding the correct prefix from the list.

prefix list	word list
un-	large
dis-	finished
re-	allow
en-	visit

Helpful hints

A **possessive pronoun** tells you who something belongs to.
For example:
• That is **my** opinion.
• They look after **their** health by eating well and exercising.
• The fruit basket is **mine.**

Sometimes we alter a word by putting a **prefix** in front of it. For example, the word 'reasonable' can be altered by adding the prefix **un-**.
• Farmers were being paid an **unreasonable** price for cocoa beans. FAIRTRADE makes sure the price they are paid is **reasonable**.

3 Write a sentence containing each of the new words from activity 2.

4 The text on page 12 has some of the techniques used to persuade the reader. Find and copy a sentence which uses personal address.

5 Think of a new title for the text on page 12 – remember it should tell you what you are going to read about. Write a new first sentence to grab the reader's attention.

Cooking healthy meals

I can use suffixes.

Simple, scrumptious recipes children will love

Inspiration for feeding a hungry family.

Teach children how to make this pasta supper – it's a tasty family meal packed with nutrients. It takes just 15 minutes to prepare and 30 minutes to cook.

Children as young as two can join in and help out. It's also a great way to teach basic division to older children while they are having fun.

As you cook, learn about the different ingredients and where they come from. The family that eats together, after they have cooked together, enjoys a happy, healthy lifestyle.

1 Read the text above. It contains **subordinating connectives**. For example: *It's also a great way to teach basic division to older children <u>while</u> they are having fun.*

Underline the subordinating connectives in these instructions to cook a pasta supper.

a The children can divide the meatballs while you stir the sauce.

b Put the pasta into the pan after the water has boiled.

c Check the children have washed their hands if they have handled the raw ingredients.

d The meal is enough for a family of four although you can add extra for a bigger family.

e Use fresh herbs for the sauce because they have better flavour.

Helpful hints

A subordinating connective allows you to extend your sentences by adding a **subordinate clause** to your main clause.

For example:

- *The boy in the red jumper arrived at school* (**main clause**) *<u>after</u>* (subordinating connective) *the bell had rung.* (subordinating clause)

- *The shop sold out of cold drinks* (**main clause**) *<u>because</u>* (subordinating connective) *the weather had been so hot.* (subordinating clause)

Looking at connectives

I can use subordinating connectives.

I can note the use of persuasive devices in text.

1 Use the root words and suffixes in the table to build as many longer words as you can. You can use the root words with more than one suffix. Be careful to change spelling when you need to.

root words	suffixes
happy sad peace home hope	-ness -ful -less -ly

Helpful hints

A **suffix** is a group of letters you add to the end of a root word to build longer words.
For example:
root word – enjoy
suffix – **-ment**
longer word – enjoyment

Can you find the root words in the table above that you can add two suffixes to?

Try this

2 The text on page 14 uses **adjectives** (describing words) to persuade. The adjectives in these sentences have been underlined. Rewrite the sentences using different adjectives.

a Inspiration for feeding a <u>hungry</u> family.

b It's a <u>tasty</u> family meal packed with nutrients.

c It's also a <u>great</u> way to teach basic division to older children.

d As you cook, learn about the <u>different</u> ingredients.

e The family that eats together, after they have cooked together, enjoys a <u>happy</u> lifestyle.

The importance of water

Drink plenty

To stay healthy and keep your body working well, you need to drink about six to eight glasses of fluid a day. Drinking plenty of fluids helps to keep you hydrated. Being well hydrated helps your body and mind work properly so you can concentrate, learn and be active.

Some drinks contain a lot of sugar and even some preservatives. These are not good for your health or your teeth. A really healthy option is water.

Do you drink water? Or do you need a bit of encouragement? Here are a few ideas to persuade you to drink more water:

- Freeze the water – it's much more fun to drink water that is thawing.
- Focus on the positive – keep a table which shows how well you are doing.
- Learn how you are helping your body by drinking water.

Did you know?

- Water is essential for life on Earth.
- It covers about 70 per cent of the Earth's surface.
- Pure water has no taste and no smell.
- Water is also used for fun. Activities include swimming, sailing, skiing and snowboarding.

I can use a dictionary to find out about specialised vocabulary.

I can prepare and present an argument to persuade others.

1 Read the text on page 16. It contains some specialised vocabulary:

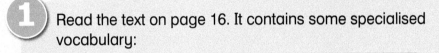

fluid   hydrated   preservatives

a Look these words up in a dictionary.
b The word hydrated comes from the root word hydrate. Use the root word to make more words using suffixes and prefixes.

Talk Partners

Discuss with a talk partner which drinks you like. Think about why you like them. Discuss how water is a healthier option.

2 How would you persuade your friends to drink more water?
Write an article for a school newsletter, using persuasive language, encouraging everyone to drink more water. Remember to use personal pronouns (such as 'you' and 'your') and to ask questions.

3 These words all have the letter string **ough** in them but are pronounced in three different ways. Pair up the words where **ough** is pronounced in the same way.

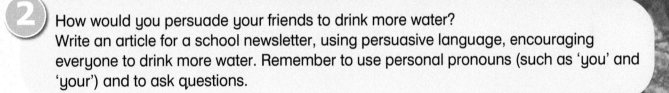

bough   dough   rough   though   enough   plough

Gardening

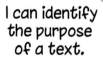

I can identify the purpose of a text.

Green fingers

Eating your greens is all the more appealing when you've helped grow them yourself! Getting involved in the garden helps you to understand where food comes from and teaches you about the different ways that fruit and vegetables grow. It's great fun to pull up your own vegetables and help to prepare and cook them.

You only need a small space to grow your own produce, even a pot will do for some plants.

If you want to start really small, fresh herbs are a nice idea. Pot up some chives and basil on your kitchen windowsill and snip them with scissors when you want to add them into recipes.

Get yourself a set of tools and a colourful pair of gloves and always make sure that you wash your hands after digging and weeding. You'll have a fantastic time!

1 Read the text above. What is the main purpose of the text?
  a   To persuade you to wash your hands?
  b   To persuade you to cook vegetables?
  c   To persuade you to grow your own fruit and vegetables?
  Find a phrase from the text which supports your answer.
  Explain how it shows this.

Persuading

> I know the spelling rules for words ending in **e** and **y**.

> I can recall and discuss important features of a talk and contribute new ideas.

1 Copy and complete this table.

I	He
fly	flies
try	
	cries
apply	
fry	

Helpful hints

Spelling rule top tip:
When a **verb** (a doing word) ends with a consonant before the letter y we take off the y and add -**ies**. For example: fly – flies.

2 Now put each of these words from activity 1 into a sentence. For example: I am going to the beach to **fly** my kite. My kite **flies** high in the sky.

Talk Partners

In pairs prepare a talk to persuade your teacher to set up a gardening club in school. Make notes for your first draft and then improve on it before presenting your ideas to the class. Think about when the gardening club will meet, where a garden could be set up in school and what would happen to any fruit or vegetables which are grown.

What have I learnt?

Check what you have learnt in this unit:
* I know the key features of a persuasive text.
* I understand the difference between a simple and complex sentence.
* I can write and punctuate direct speech.
* I can write my own persuasive text.

2 Stories from other cultures

Mufaro's Beautiful Daughters

A long time ago, in a certain place in Africa there was a small village. It was a half day's journey from the city where a great king lived. A man named Mufaro lived in this village with his two daughters, who were called Manyara and Nyasha. Everyone agreed that Manyara and Nyasha were very beautiful.

Manyara was almost always in a bad temper. She teased her sister when their father's back was turned and she had been heard to say, "Someday, Nyasha, I will be a queen and you will be a servant in my household."

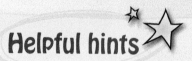

Helpful hints

A **narrative** text is written to tell a story. This is an extract from a traditional African folktale, set in Zimbabwe, originally passed down by word of mouth.

"If that should come to pass," Nyasha responded, "I will be pleased to serve you. But why do you say such things? Why are you so unhappy?"

"Because everyone talks about how kind you are, and they praise everything you do," Manyara replied. "I'm certain that Father loves you best. But when I am a queen, everyone will know that your silly kindness is only weakness."

Nyasha was sad that Manyara felt this way, but she ignored her sister's words and went about her chores. Nyasha worked on a small plot of land, on which she grew millet, sunflowers, yams and vegetables. Many creatures were attracted to the garden. One morning, Nyasha noticed a small garden snake resting beneath a yam vine. "Good day, little Nyoka," she called to him, "You are welcome here. You will keep away any creatures who might spoil my vegetables." The garden flourished and time passed.

One day a messenger from the big city arrived. "The most Worthy and Beautiful Daughters in the Land are invited to appear before the King." That was the message.

From Mufaro's Beautiful Daughters *by John Steptoe*

I can comment on the writer's choice of language.

I know how characters are presented in a story.

1 Read the extract on page 20 and find the evidence to support these characteristics for Manyara, Nyasha and their father Mufaro. Copy and complete the table.

Name	Characteristic	Evidence
Manyara	unkind jealous	
Nyasha	kind forgiving	
Mufaro	proud	

2 **a** Identify the unstressed vowel in the underlined words below.

> The <u>family</u> lived in a small village. Manyara was often <u>miserable</u>. Nyasha grew <u>marvellous</u> vegetables in her garden. The little snake was not <u>poisonous.</u>

b Think of a word with an unstressed vowel and put it into a sentence.

Helpful hints

Some words have **unstressed vowels** in them. These are vowels (a, e, i, o, u) that are not easy to hear in a word. For example, *we like <u>different</u> books*. The first vowel, i, is stressed. It is easy to hear. The letter e after the f is unstressed – it is not easy to hear.

Talk Partners

With your partner take the part of two siblings (brothers and sisters). Decide which of you will be like Manyara and which will be like Nyasha. Work together to make a small play where you act your characters. Perform this to the rest of your class.

> I know how characters are presented in a story.

> I understand how connectives can be used to show opposites.

More about Mufaro's daughters

1 Read the text on page 20 again. Identify which of the characters in the story would do these actions:

a Convinces father that she alone should go to meet the king.

b Rushes away early in the morning hoping to arrive at the palace first.

c Leaves home reluctantly.

d Refuses to help a hungry, small child who asks for food.

e Offers food to a small, hungry child walking in the forest.

f Ignores the advice given by an old woman sitting by the side of the road.

g Listens to the advice given by an old woman sitting by the side of the road.

h Sings 'I will be queen' to herself as she travels to the city.

Helpful hints

A **synopsis** is a brief summary of something. Here is a synopsis of the story of Mufaro's daughters.

> Mufaro's two beautiful daughters are very different. One, Manyara, is cunning and unkind. The other, Nyasha, is polite and kind. The king from a nearby city sends a message that all of the beautiful daughters in his kingdom are to go to his palace.

Connectives can be used to show that two things are 'opposite' to each other. For example: *Manyara left when it was still dark **but** Nyasha waited until it was light.*

2 These sentences show opposites. Choose the best connective from the brackets to link them.

a Manyara refused to give the hungry child any food (because/unlike) Nyasha who gave him a yam she had grown in the garden.

b Nyasha listened carefully to the old woman (whereas/likewise) Manyara ignored her advice.

c Father and Nyasha travelled to the city together (however/since) Manyara left early and went alone.

d The snake frightened Manyara (whenever/however) Nyasha laughed when she saw him.

e Nyasha knew she would miss her family and friends (and/whilst) Manyara did not worry about leaving home.

3 Write a sentence of your own, using a connective, which contrasts the two girls' actions.

The story continues

This is an extract from further into the story 'Mufaro's Beautiful Daughters'.

As Mufaro and Nyasha approached the city they saw Manyara running towards them. She was shaking and snuffling, and clutched at her family.

"Do not go to the king, my sister" she babbled, talking on and on of a snake with five heads who recited her faults to her and made her cower. Nyasha was scared, but she had come this far, and would see what fortune brought her. Mufaro watched while his younger child went bravely to the door of the king's chamber.

With trepidation, she opened the door, and, as her eyes adjusted to the dim light, she burst out giggling with relief. Indeed there was a snake: her little friend, Nyoka.

"Why are you here?" the girl asked. And he replied, "I am the king," and transformed into a handsome young man. Gold bracelets encircled his bare arms.

"I am the king. I am also the hungry boy with whom you shared a yam in the forest and the old woman you listened to and gave some seeds to. But you know me best as Nyoka. Because I have been all of these, I know you to be the Most Worthy and Most Beautiful Daughter in the Land. It would make me very happy if you would be my wife."

From Mufaro's Beautiful Daughters *by John Steptoe*

Glossary

recited: said aloud
trepidation: a feeling of fear

I can skim read to get a general idea of the story content.

I can scan for specific detail.

1 Which of these reading strategies would you use to find out about these statements?

Statement		Skim	Scan
a	Manyara felt very upset.		
b	Nyoka had been many characters throughout the story.		
c	The prince wore gold bracelets.		
d	Nyasha was kind to everyone she met.		

Helpful hints

Skim reading gives you a general idea of the story. You read quickly and miss out on the details in the text.
Scan reading gives you the opportunity to pick up on particular details. You search for key words or ideas to answer a question you may have.

Talk Partners

Manyara told her father that a snake with many heads recited her many faults to her. Talk with your partner about Manyara's faults and think about what you would say to her about her faults if you met her. Practise saying these, supporting each one with evidence.

2 Write down what the snake would have said to Manyara. Use direct speech, remember to punctuate it and support each point with evidence. For example:
The snake said, "Manyara, you are selfish because you would not share your food with a hungry boy."

Helpful hints

In a sentence the subject and verb must agree or the sentence does not make sense. For example: *The children* (subject) *sang* (verb) *at the party.*

3 Work out what is wrong in these sentences. Rewrite them so that they make sense.
  a When Nyasha see the snake she giggled.
  b Nyoka were not a snake at all.
  c The handsome prince asking Nyasha to marry him.
  d Mufaro were a very proud man.
  e The king wear gold bracelets on his arms.

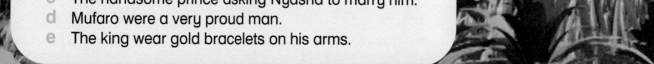

The happy ending

Here is the ending to the story.

The preparations for the wedding were made, and Nyasha herself baked the marriage bread, of millet harvested from her own garden, rich with the love of her home. As for Mufaro, he lived happily ever after. Why not? He had two beautiful daughters, one of whom was queen... and the other, a servant in the queen's household!

Helpful hints

At the start of the story one daughter was sure she would be queen and the other her servant. There is a **twist** at the end of this story. This means things did not turn out as expected.

1 Copy and complete these sentences.
   a   At the start of the story Mufaro was a happy man, Manyara thought _____ and that Nyasha _____.

   b   At the end of the story Mufaro was a happy man, Nyasha _____ and Manyara _____.

Talk Partners   Talk with your partner about the characters in the story. Think about how another character could be introduced, perhaps another character for Nyoka to become or perhaps a step-mother who supports Manyara. Think of how that character would change the story, what they would do and how others would react.

2 Write a section of the story that has your new character in it.

Helpful hints

An **adverb** tells the reader more about the verb. A good example of this is when you are describing how someone speaks. For example:
"Hello little snake, welcome to my garden," Nyasha said (**verb**) *gently* (**adverb**).

3 Copy and complete the sentences. Select an adverb from the box so that the reader knows how the character spoke.

| happily   proudly   angrily   boastfully   gently |

   a   "Father loves you the most!" Manyara shouted _____.
   b   "I will be queen," Manyara said _____. "You will be my servant."
   c   "My two daughters are beautiful," Mufaro boasted _____ .
   d   "You look hungry, have this yam from my garden," Nyasha whispered _____.
   e   "I will be pleased to marry you," Nyasha answered _____ .

25

A story from Johannesburg

This is an extract from the book *Journey to Jo'burg* by Beverley Naidoo. Two children, Naledi and Tiro, decide that they must try to find their mother in Johannesburg, where she works, as their baby sister is very ill.

The children went to find Naledi's friend Poleng, and explained. Poleng was very surprised but agreed to help. She would tell Nono once the children had gone and she also promised to help their granny, bringing the water and doing the other jobs.

"How will you eat on the way?" Poleng asked.

Tiro looked worried but Naledi was confident.

"Oh, we'll find something."

Poleng told them to wait and ran into her house, returning soon with a couple of sweet potatoes and a bottle of water. The children thanked her. She was indeed a good friend.

Before they could go, Naledi had to get the last letter Mma had sent, so they would know where to look for her in the big city. Slipping into the house, Naledi took the letter from the tin without Nono or Mmangwane noticing. Both were busy with Dineo as Naledi slipped out again.

The children walked quickly away from the village. The road was really just a track made by car tyres. Two lines of dusty red earth leading out across the flat, dry grassland.

Once at the big tar road, they turned in the direction of the early morning sun, for that was the way to Johannesburg. The steel railway line glinted alongside the road.

From Journey to Jo'burg *by Beverley Naidoo*

Did you know?

This story is set in South Africa at a time when different groups of people were kept separate from each other. This was called apartheid. Nelson Mandela was a leading figure in the fight against apartheid which has now been abolished.

Helpful hints

To work out what is happening in a story you have to read very carefully and look for **evidence** that supports your opinions.

1 Read the extract on page 26 again then answer these questions. Provide evidence which supports your answers. Copy and complete the table.

Question	Answer	Evidence
Who do the children live with?		
Why does Poleng need to bring water after they have left?		
How did Naledi manage to get her mother's address?		
Were the children prepared for the journey?		

2 Which of the two children is more confident about the trip ahead? How does the writer tell you this?

Writing presentation

Imagine you are part of Naledi and Tiro's family and are joining them on the trip to find their mother. Write the part of the story when you are planning the trip as if you are writing a diary. Remember to write in first person (I, my) and to include how you feel about what is happening and your worries. Afterwards, check through your story and underline any words that are spelt incorrectly. Write these words in your spelling journal and practise spelling them correctly.

3 The story *Journey to Jo'burg* has sentences which use commas to separate clauses. For example: 'Once at the big tar road, they turned in the direction of the early morning sun, for that was the way to Johannesburg.' Write out the sentences below, putting a comma in the correct places.

Helpful hints

Using a **comma** lets the reader take a pause and helps clarify the meaning of a sentence.

a The grass was dry and scratchy but they were used to it.

b Now and again a car or a truck roared by and then the road went quiet again and they were alone.

c Their legs slowed down as they began to walk uphill their bodies feeling heavy.

d The long road ahead stretched into the distance between fenced-off fields and dry grass up to another hill.

More about the journey

The children are offered shelter for the night and then manage to get a ride on a lorry going to Johannesburg, over 250 km away. Once in Johannesburg they wait for a bus to take them to where their mother lives.

Luckily the bus wasn't full when it arrived. Grace had warned them that in the rush hour you were almost squeezed to death. As the bus trundled along, stopping and starting with the traffic there was a chance to stare out of the windows. Tiro thought the cyclists were very brave, riding in between all the cars. Nadeli kept trying to see the tops of the tall buildings, twisting her neck around until it began to hurt.

The bus now heaved its way up a steep hill and soon they were leaving the city buildings, seeing the sky again, as well as trees, grass lawns and flowers either side of the road. Behind the trees were big houses, such as they had never seen before.

Extract from Journey to Jo'burg *by Beverley Naidoo.*

1

a Read the extract above. In it the writer says 'Grace had warned them that in the rush hour you were almost squeezed to death.' Write this as if Grace actually spoke the words.

b She also wrote 'Tiro thought the cyclists were very brave.' Write this as if Tiro actually spoke the words.

2 As the journey progresses the children find themselves in very different places. Match the descriptions below to where they are. Copy and complete the table.

Description	Where they are
Kept trying to see the tops of the tall buildings.	
Behind the trees were big houses, such as they had never seen before.	

Helpful hints

We use **inverted commas** to show when someone is speaking in a text. They separate the speech from the rest of the text. For example: *"You can stay in the barn tonight,"* offered the young boy.*

Remember:
- To use a comma before the closing speech marks and a full stop at the end of the sentence.
- To use speech marks for direct speech. Look back to the Helpful hints box on page 11 to remind yourself.

A worrying time

The children become separated from Grace and are involved in an incident which frightens them.

Suddenly, without any warning, there was a commotion up ahead. Three figures in uniform stood at the top of the stairs.

Police!

People began turning around and coming rapidly back down. Some were running along the platform towards a high barbed-wire fence at the other end. The runners leapt at the fence and scrambled over it.

Others jumped down to the track, sprinted over the railway lines and clambered up to the opposite platform. But just as they got there, more policemen appeared on that side.

"Where can we go?" Tiro urgently tugged at his sister's hand.

"We'll have to slip past them," she whispered, pulling him towards the stairs.

Some people were feeling into pockets, others frantically searching through bags.

Pass raid!

A man was protesting loudly that he had left his pass at home. It would take only two minutes to get it. The police could come and see, or someone could call his child to bring it. He cried out the address once, twice … Slap!

Extract from Journey to Jo'burg *by Beverley Naidoo.*

1 Read the extract above. Write out these sentences and underline the adverb in each one.

  a People began turning around and coming rapidly back down.

  b Some people were feeling into pockets, others frantically searching through bags.

  c A man was protesting loudly that he had left his pass at home.

  d "Where can we go?" Tiro urgently tugged at his sister's hand.

  e The crowd were running across the track quickly.

Helpful hints

In this extract the writer has used **adverbs** to help build up the feeling of danger and tension. An adverb gives the reader more information about the verb. For example: Everyone **looked** (verb) **anxiously** (adverb) around. An adverb tells you how, when or where the action is taking place.

Explain why the writer has written one and two word sentences in this extract, such as:
Police!
Pass raid!

Try this

> I can describe events.

> I can ask questions to learn more about an event.

Describing an event

Talk Partners

With a partner write down the adverbs from activity 1 on page 29 and say them out loud. Think about the tone of voice – you need to show the sense of danger which the writer wanted to create. Think of some more adverbs which you could use in these situations and take turns to say them out loud. Add some actions and present this to the rest of the class.

Writing presentation

Imagine you are one of the passengers from the train. You spot the police as you get off and you begin searching for your pass. Write about how you are feeling, what you are doing, what else is going on around you and who else is with you. Remember to use paragraphs. Include some of the adverbs from the Talk Partners activity above.

1 The facts in the Did you know? box about Nelson Mandela give a very brief overview of his life. Copy and complete the table below to help you write down questions which would help you to find out more about him.

Family life	
School life	
Life fighting apartheid	
Life in prison	
Life as the President	

Did you know?

Nelson Mandela is known as the man who changed the world. He was born in 1918 and was the first member of his family to go to school. In 1952 he set up a law firm which represented black people in South Africa. He always argued against apartheid but in the 1960s he began to fight against the strict rules which separated the different races who lived in South Africa. He escaped from the police on many occasions by disguising himself as a fieldworker, a chauffeur and a chef. He spent 26 years in prison. Following his release in 1990 he became the President of South Africa. He worked hard to bring peace to his country.

Fly, Eagle, Fly!

Fly, Eagle, Fly! is an African tale. The story starts as a farmer goes out searching for a lost calf.

He climbed up a gully in case the calf had huddled there to escape the storm. And that was where he stopped. For there, on a ledge of rock, close enough to touch, he saw the most unusual sight – an eagle chick, very young, hatched from its egg a day or two before and then blown from its nest by the terrible storm.

He reached out and cradled it in both hands. He would take it home and care for it. And home he went, still calling, calling in case the calf might hear.

He was almost home when the children ran out to meet him. "The calf came home by itself!" they shouted. He was very pleased. He showed the eagle chick to his wife and children, then placed it carefully in the warm kitchen under the watchful eye of the roosters.

"The eagle is king of the birds," he said, "but we shall train it to be a chicken."

So the eagle lived among the chickens, learning their ways. His children called their friends to see the strange bird. For as it grew, living on the bits and pieces put out for the chickens, it began to look quite different from any chicken they had ever seen.

One day a friend dropped by for a visit. The friend saw the bird among the chickens. "Hey! That's not a chicken. It's an eagle!"

The farmer smiled at him and said, "Of course it's a chicken. Look – it walks like a chicken, it talks like a chicken. Of course it's a chicken."

But the friend was not convinced. "I will show you that it is an eagle," he said.

"Go ahead," said the farmer.

From Fly, Eagle, Fly! *retold by Christopher Gregorowski*

1

> He was very pleased. He showed the eagle chick to his wife and children, then placed it carefully in the warm kitchen under the watchful eye of the roosters.

Read the extract above. In this section of the story we hear that the farmer presents the eagle chick to his family. Write this section to show what the farmer and his family would say to each other. For example: "Children, come here quickly. Look what I found when I was searching for the calf," the farmer called to his children. Continue this conversation until the chick is settled with the hens and the family leave to do their chores around the farm.

Talk Partners

Share your dialogue with a partner. Can you work out what each character feels about the chick from the way they speak? Work together to show each character's reaction.

Writing techniques

1 Copy and complete these sentences with a word which sounds similar to the word underlined.

 a   The baby chick was blown down by the <u>gale</u> and hit by falling _____.

 b   The farmer put the chick in the <u>pen</u> with a _____.

 c   When the <u>friend</u> visited he could not _____ the eagle was a chicken.

 d   The lost calf <u>found</u> its way home safe and _____.

 e   The eagle did not <u>walk</u> like a chicken and it did not _____ like a chicken.

2 The farmer is the key character in this part of the story. He carries out most of the actions. Copy and complete this table to show what his motives are. Remember to back this up with evidence. The first one has been done for you.

Action	Feelings	Motive
looked for the calf	*anxious, concerned*	*wanted to make the calf safe as there was a storm*
reached out for the chick		
placed the chick carefully in the warm kitchen		
trained the eagle to be a chicken		
smiled at his friend and said, "Of course it is a chicken."		

3 Change the underlined words in these sentences into plurals.

 a   The farmer was worried the <u>wolf</u> would attack the baby calf.

 b   The farmer was worried the wolf would attack the baby <u>calf</u>.

 c   The storm had caused the <u>leaf</u> to fall from the trees.

 d   When his friend arrived he split the coconut into two <u>half</u>.

 e   While it grew dark he lit the light and placed it on the <u>shelf</u>.

Helpful hints

Writers use different ways to help the reader picture what they are writing about. Sometimes they use words which sound similar. This is called **assonance**. For example: 'fleet feet', 'weeping while she was sweeping', 'walks and talks'.

A **motive** is the reason why you do something. Writers sometimes expect their readers to think about the character's motive in a text. For example:

The swimmer got up early every morning to practise for the race.

The swimmer's motive (reason for getting up early) was that he wanted to win the race.

When we want to write about more than one we have to make the word into a **plural**. For words that end in the letter **f** the usual spelling rule is to take away the **f** and add **-ves**.

Films and plays

I can write a play script.

Helpful hints

All stories can be turned into films and plays. The characters speak (dialogue) and carry out actions (stage directions). For example:

This story:
It was a hot day, the sun was shining. Ushma had a bottle of cold, refreshing water. Her brother, Aziz, was chasing after a butterfly. He spotted her drinking from the bottle.
"Oh, can I have some water, I'm really hot and thirsty?" he said.
"You know I have a bottle for you in my bag, I'll get it for you," replied Ushma.

Becomes this play:
Characters: Ushma, Aziz
Scene: A park. It is very sunny. Ushma is drinking water. Aziz is running around.
Aziz: Can I have some water, I'm really hot and thirsty?
Ushma: You know I have a bottle for you in my bag. I'll get it for you.
(Ushma reaches for her bag and takes out a bottle of water)
Aziz: Thank you Ushma.
(Aziz drinks the water)

Talk Partners

With a partner choose a part of the story from page 31 to turn into a scene from a play. Write down who the characters will be and where the play will be set.

Writing presentation

Write the section of the story you have chosen as a play. With your talk partner perform the play to the rest of the class. Afterwards, check through your story and underline any words that are spelt incorrectly. Write these words in your spelling journal and practise spelling them correctly.

Rising with the Sun

The two men set off disappearing into the darkness. They went into the valley and crossed the river, the friend leading the way. The bird was very heavy and too large to carry comfortably, but the friend insisted on taking it himself.

"Hurry," he said, "or the dawn will arrive before we do!"

The first light crept into the sky as they began to climb the mountain. Below them they could see the river snaking like a long, thin ribbon through the golden grasslands, the forest and the veld, stretching down toward the sea. The wispy clouds in the sky were pink at first and then began to shimmer with a golden brilliance.

Sometimes their path was dangerous as it clung to the side of the mountain, crossing narrow shelves of rock and taking them into dark crevices and out again. They were both panting, especially the friend who was carrying the bird.

At last he said, "This will do." He looked down the cliff and saw the ground thousands of feet below. They were very near the top.

"Look at the sun, Eagle. And when it rises, rise with it. You belong to the sky, not to the earth."

At that moment the sun's first rays shot out over the mountain, and suddenly the world was ablaze with light.

From Fly, Eagle, Fly! *retold by Christopher Gregorowski*

Talk Partners

Read the extract above. Talk with a partner about the story *Fly, Eagle, Fly!* Think about the way in which an animal has been used to demonstrate a human situation. Prepare an explanation of the story together and present it to the class as a pair, with one taking the story in sections and the other explaining the way it shows life for people. Use this table to help you.

Person 1 – the story	Person 2 – the explanation
A farmer found a baby eagle chick which had been blown out of its nest by a gale. He took it home to look after it.	People are kind, they look after those in trouble and need.
He put it in with the chickens. "The eagle is king of the birds" he said, "but we shall turn it into a chicken."	

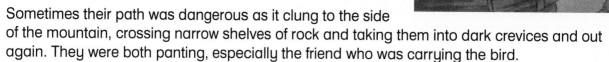

Did you know?

Archbishop Desmond Tutu, a religious leader in South Africa, wrote a message at the start of *Fly, Eagle, Fly!* 'We are not mere chickens but eagles destined to soar to great heights. We should be trying to become what we have in us to become; to gaze at the rising sun and lift off and soar.'

I can apply the rule for doubling consonants.

Spelling rules

Helpful hints

The letters a, e , i, o, u, are vowels. All of the other letters in the alphabet are **consonants**. Sometimes we need to add **-ed** or **-ing** to a word that ends in a consonant. The rule for doing this is quite tricky. Remember that we double the final letter when a one-syllable verb ends in consonant + vowel + consonant.

For example: 'rub' becomes 'rubbed' or 'rubbing'.

- Rub yourself dry with a towel.
- He rubbed himself dry with a towel.
- He is rubbing himself dry with a towel.

To make things a little more complicated we do not do this when the word ends in two consonants. For example: walk becomes walked and walking.

We do not double the letter 'w' or 'y' at the end of any words.

1 Apply the rule to these words. Copy and complete these sentences with the missing words.

a He will stop work after tea.

He _____ work after tea.

He is _____ work after tea.

b The music will start in a few minutes.

The music is _____ in a few minutes.

The music _____ a few minutes ago.

c The concert will begin at 7 o'clock

The concert is _____ at 7 o'clock.

d The cats play together in the morning.

The cats _____ together this morning.

The cats are _____ together this morning.

e People train hard to run in marathons.

People who are _____ in marathons must train hard.

The chicken becomes an eagle

All was silent. Nothing moved. The eagle's head stretched up; its wings stretched outwards; its legs leaned forward as its claws clutched the rock.

And then, without really moving, feeling the updraft of a wind more powerful than any man or bird, the great eagle leaned forward and was swept upward, higher and higher, lost to sight in the brightness of the rising sun, never again to live among the chickens.

From Fly, Eagle, Fly! *retold by Christopher Gregorowski*

1 Read the extract above. The writer uses alliteration in this final section of the text. He writes 'its **legs leaned** forward as its **claws clutched** the rock.'
Copy these sentences and underline the alliteration.

a Did you shine your shoes today?   b The colourful kites soared high in the sky.
c He waved warily as the car drove away.   d The sloth slithered across the lawn.

Talk Partners

The two stories *Journey from Jo'burg* and *Fly, Eagle, Fly!* have a common theme. Talk with your partner about what these two stories have in common and what is different about them. Copy this table to help you. Remember to include evidence from the text.

Theme	*Journey to Jo'burg*	*Fly, Eagle, Fly!*
A difficult journey	The children travel from home to where their mother works.	They went into the valley and crossed the river.

What have I learnt?

Check what you have learnt in this unit:
* I understand how characters are presented in a story.
* I can introduce a new character in a story.
* I can recognise and use adverbs to improve my writing.
* I can turn a story into a playscript.

Unit 3 Poems that tell a story

Chocolate cake

Anyway,
Once we had this chocolate cake for tea
and later I went to bed
but while I was in bed
I found myself waking up
licking my lips
and smiling.
I woke up proper.
'The chocolate cake'.
It was the first thing I thought of.

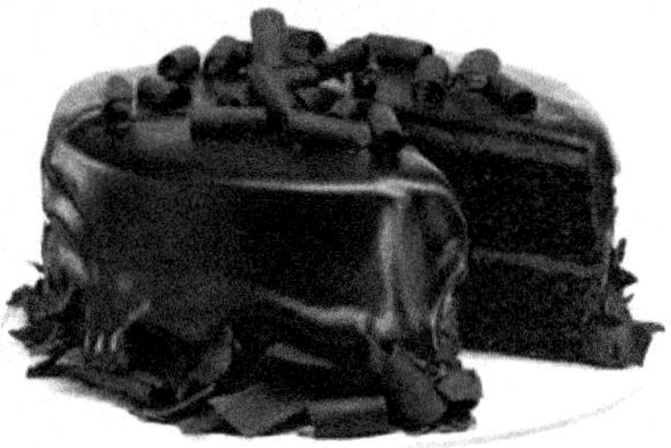

I could almost see it
so I thought
what if I go downstairs
and have a little nibble, yeah?

It was all dark
everyone was in bed
so it must have been really late
but I got out of bed
crept out of the door

there's always a creaky floorboard isn't there?

past Mum and Dad's room,
careful not to tread on any bits of broken toys
or bits of Lego
with your bare feet

yowwww
shhhhhhh

From Chocolate cake *by Michael Rosen*

Helpful hints

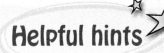

This is an extract (part of) a poem about how much the writer loves chocolate cake. It is written by Michael Rosen.

Did you know?

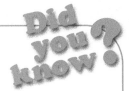

Michael Rosen lives in London. He is one of the most popular writers of poetry for children. He started writing when he was just 15 years old. He uses his own experiences, and everyday activities like brushing your teeth, to write poems which children understand and like.

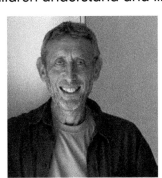

I can identify the plot in a narrative poem.

I can perform a narrative poem.

I can identify the point of view from which a poem is written.

1 Read the poem on page 37. Which of these statements give us clues that tell us the writer knows he is doing something his parents would not like?

a   The writer likes chocolate cake.
b   The writer woke up.
c   All the writer can think about is the cake downstairs.
d   The writer crept past his parents' room.
e   The writer had bare feet.

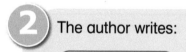

Talk Partners

With a partner read the poem on page 37 aloud. Remember to use the actions given in the poem and add some of your own. Perform the poem to the rest of the class.

Helpful hints

Poems that tell a story are called **narrative** poems. The key features of narrative poems are:

- the author has a story to tell
- there is a plot which develops throughout the poem
- the author has a point of view which the reader is made aware of.

2 The author writes:

> yowwww
> shhhhhhh

a   Can you explain what has happened in the poem at this point?
b   Mime this part of the poem, do not use any words at all. Show what is happening using actions only.

I know what a preposition is.

I can use a preposition in my own writing.

Looking at prepositions

1 Write out these sentences and underline the prepositions.

a Mum made chocolate cake for our tea.
b There was some cake left over after tea.
c I remembered there was some chocolate cake in the kitchen.
d I crept downstairs, avoiding the toys on the floor.
e The knife was near the cake tin.

2 Make up a sentence of your own about something you like very much using a preposition. Underline the preposition in your sentence.

Talk Partners

With a talk partner make a list of five place prepositions, five time prepositions and five direction prepositions. Challenge each other to make a sentence which contains one of the different types of prepositions.

Helpful hints

A **preposition** tells you where the **subject** of the sentence is. It can tell you the place. For example:

* *The <u>sun</u> (subject) shone brightly <u>in</u> (preposition) the sky.*

It can tell you the time. For example:

* *<u>Matéo</u> (subject) went swimming <u>before</u> (preposition) supper.*

It can tell you direction. For example:

* *The new <u>path</u> (subject) has been built <u>along</u> (preposition) the river.*

More about Chocolate cake

In the morning I get up
downstairs
have breakfast,
Mum's saying
'Have you got your dinner money?'
and I say,
'Yes'
'And don't forget to take some chocolate cake with you.'
I stopped breathing.

'What's the matter,' she says,
'you normally jump at chocolate cake.'

I'm still not breathing
and she's looking at me very close now.

She's looking at me just below my mouth.
'What's that?' she says.
'What's what?' I say

'What's that there?'
'Where?'
'There,' she says, pointing at my chin.
'I don't know,' I say.
'It looks like chocolate,' she says
'It's not chocolate is it?'
No answer.
'Is it?'
'I don't know.'
She goes to the cupboard
looks in, up, top, middle, bottom
turns back to me
'It's gone.
It's gone.
You haven't eaten it have you?'
'I don't know.'
'You don't know. You don't know if you've eaten a whole chocolate cake or not?'
'When? When did you eat it?'

So I told her.

From Chocolate cake *by Michael Rosen*

Silent letters

I can describe events.

I can identify silent letters in words.

Talk Partners

Work with a partner to read these words aloud:

> business   scissors   fasten
>   different   interest

Copy the words out and underline the letters which are silent.

Helpful hints

The word 'chocolate' has a **silent letter** in it. Silent letters are letters that you can't hear when you say a word. They are there when you spell the word.

There are lots of words with silent letters in them, such as i**s**land, dou**b**t, thum**b** and lam**b**.

1

Read the poem on page 40. This extract tells of the moment when Mum realises the cake has been eaten. There are two characters, Mum and the narrator.

Copy and complete this table with words which show how each character's feelings change as the story unfolds.

Mum	Narrator

Mum's story

I can write from another viewpoint.

I can collect synonyms and opposites and investigate shades of meaning.

Talk Partners

Talk with your partner about how Mum felt when she realised the chocolate cake had been eaten. How did she know and what did she do about it?

1 Rewrite the section of the poem on page 40 where Mum becomes suspicious, this time writing it from her point of view. Remember to think about the style the poem is written in, use short lines and put inverted commas around any speech.

Helpful hints

A **synonym** is a word with the same, or a very similar, meaning to another word. For example, you could write:
- The door was closed.
- The door was shut.

Closed and shut mean the same thing in this sentence.

Talk Partners

Read your version of the poem to your partner. Make suggestions to improve each other's poems.

Try this

Read your version of the poem out to the rest of the class. Use your talk partner as the child who ate the cake. Remember to include the actions which could go with this section of the poem.

2 Give a synonym for each of the following words, which the writer has used in the poem. Copy and complete the table.

word	synonym
normally	
gone	
answer	
whole	

The tale of Custard the Dragon

Belinda lived in a little white house,
With a little black kitten and a little grey mouse,
And a little yellow dog and a little red wagon,
And a realio, trulio, little pet dragon.

Now the name of the little black kitten was Ink,
And the little grey mouse, she called her Blink,
And the little yellow dog was sharp as Mustard,
But the dragon was a coward, and she called him Custard.

Custard the dragon had big sharp teeth,
And spikes on top of him and scales underneath,
Mouth like a fireplace, chimney for a nose,
And realio, trulio, daggers on his toes.

Belinda was as brave as a barrel full of bears,
And Ink and Blink chased lions down the stairs,
Mustard was as brave as a tiger in a rage,
But Custard cried for a nice safe cage.

Belinda tickled him, she tickled him unmerciful,
Ink, Blink and Mustard, they rudely called him Percival,
They all sat laughing in the little red wagon
At the realio, trulio, cowardly dragon.

Belinda giggled till she shook the house,
And Blink said Week!, which is giggling for a mouse,
Ink and Mustard rudely asked his age,
When Custard cried for a nice safe cage.

From Custard the Dragon *by Ogden Nash*

Glossary

realio, trulio: the author has played with the words 'real' and 'true'

unmerciful: cruel and ruthless, showing no mercy

I can use rhyming words.

I can identify how characters are presented.

Looking at language

1 Read the poem on page 43. Turn these similes from the poem into metaphors.

a The little yellow dog was sharp as mustard.

b Belinda was as brave as a barrel full of bears.

c Mustard was as brave as a tiger in a rage.

Writing presentation

Create your own story poem using the same patterning as *Custard the Dragon*. Think about the characters that will be in it. Think about the characteristics that animals have in stories. For example, dragons are seen as fearless; the owl is seen as wise; the tortoise is seen as slow. Change these characteristics to their opposites in your poem.

Use the poem *Custard the Dragon* as a template, putting four lines in every verse with each pair of lines ending with rhyming words and repeating a pattern of words for the last lines.

Jot down some rhyming words to help you get started – For example, '*wall/tall*' '*giraffe/laugh*', '*bird/heard*', '*wise/surprise*', '*clown/frown*'.

⭐ Helpful hints

The writer has used lots of different ways to describe the characters in the poem on page 43. He has used **similes**. A simile is when something is described as being 'as' or 'like' something else. For example '*mouth like a fireplace*'.

A **metaphor** compares two things directly.

For example:

- *The moon was like a misty shadow* (**simile**).
- *The moon was a misty shadow* (**metaphor**).

The poet has used **repetition**. For example, '*realio, trulio*' in every other verse.

Try this

When you have finished read your poem aloud to the rest of the class – remember to use lots of expression.

Sun is laughing

This morning she got up
On the happy side of the bed,
Pulled back
The grey sky-curtains
And poked her head
Through the blue window
Of heaven,
Her yellow laughter
Spilling over,
Falling broad across the grass,
Brightening the washing line,
Giving more shine
To the back of a ladybug
And buttering up all the world.

Then, without any warning,
As if she was suddenly bored,
Or just got sulky
Because she could hear no one
Giving praise
To her shining ways,
Sun slammed the sky-window closed,
Plunging the whole world
Into greyness once more.
O Sun, moody one,
How can we live
Without the holiday of your face?

By Grace Nichols

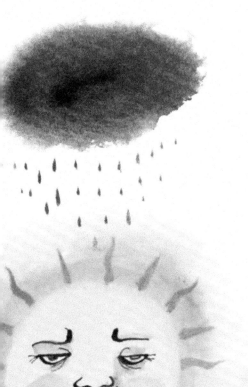

Talk Partners

Read the poem on page 45 together and discuss what happens from when 'she got up' to when 'the whole world' was grey. Write down the moods which the sun goes through from the beginning to the end of the poem. With your partner practise reading the poem out loud using movement and gestures to show the sun's actions.

Helpful hints

Personification is a technique writers use to give human qualities to objects or animals. In this poem personification is used to show the sun as a person. For example: 'poked her head through the blue window'.

1 Copy and complete this table to show what the poet means with words she has chosen. One has been done for you.

Poet's words	Meaning
grey sky-curtains	
Brightening the washing line	
buttering up all the world	*treating everyone nicely*
slammed the sky-window closed	
Without the holiday of your face	

What have I learnt?

Check what you have learnt in this unit:
- I understand the key features of a narrative poem.
- I can perform a poem with actions.
- I understand the writer's point of view and can rewrite a story from another point of view.
- I can see where a poet has used different language techniques for effect such as similes, metaphors and personification and can use these in my own writing.

Fiction

Read the story and answer ALL the questions which follow.

Anansi and the pot of wisdom

A long time ago, Anansi the spider had all the wonderful wisdom in the world stored in a huge pot. He had been given it by Nyame, the sky god. Anansi had been told to share the precious wisdom with everyone. Every day, he looked in the pot, and learned something new. The pot was full of amazing ideas and new skills.

Anansi was greedy. He said to himself, "I won't share this amazing treasure of knowledge with everyone. I will keep it all to myself."

So, Anansi decided to hide the wisdom in the topmost branches of a tall tree. He got some vines to make strong rope which he tied firmly around the pot, leaving one end free. Then he tied the loose end around his waist so that the pot hung in front of him. He started to climb the tree. He really struggled to climb as the pot of wisdom kept getting in his way, bumping against him as he climbed.

Anansi's young son watched, fascinated as his father struggled up the tree. Finally, Anansi's son called out to him loudly, "Why not tie the pot to your back, it will be so much easier for you to hold on to the tree as you climb."

So Anansi tied the pot to his back instead and continued to climb the tree, finding the task much easier than before. When Anansi got to the top of the tree, he became angry, "My young son used common sense. He was so much cleverer than me yet I have the pot of wisdom."

Furiously Anansi threw the pot of wisdom down from the tree. It smashed to pieces and shards of wisdom scattered in every direction. People found the splinters scattered everywhere, and if they wanted to, they could take a fragment home to their families and friends. That is why to this day, no one person has ALL the world's wisdom. People everywhere share small pieces of it whenever they exchange ideas.

Adapted by Anne Basden

1   How would you describe Anansi's behaviour when he decided to keep all the   (1)
    wisdom to himself? Choose the correct answer.
    a   He was being unselfish.
    b   He was being careful.
    c   He was being selfish.
    d   He was being foolish.

2   Find and write the words Anansi uses which support your answer to question 1.   (1)

3   In the first paragraph the writer has used words which tell you how important   (3)
    the wisdom was. Write them down.

4   Find and write the phrase which tells you that Anansi's son found what his   (1)
    father was doing interesting.

5   Which word tells us that Anansi's son watched his father struggle for a long time?   (1)

6   Anansi spoke these words: (1)

    "I won't share this amazing treasure of knowledge with everyone.
    I will keep it all to myself."

    Change the words into reported speech.

7   Why did Anansi get angry?   (1)

8   Explain why it was more sensible for Anansi to climb with the pot on his back.   (1)

9   Find and write the sentence that tells you that the smashing of the pot has had   (1)
    an impact on people today.

10 Underline the subordinate clause in these sentences.   (3)
    a   People everywhere share small pieces of it whenever they exchange ideas.
    b   He was so much cleverer than me yet I have the pot of wisdom.
    c   He got some vines to make strong rope which he tied firmly around the pot,
        leaving one end free.

11 The writer has written 'the wonderful wisdom in the world'. Name the technique   (2)
    used here and say why the writer has used it.

12 Write the story from Anansi's son's viewpoint.   (5)
    You will need to set the scene, explaining what the importance of the pot is and how
    Anansi came to have it.

    You will need to show:
    •   What he sees from the bottom of the tree.
    •   What he does to help his father.
    •   What happens at the end.

    You will need to think about:
    •   the language you will use, for example, how to show a character is speaking.

Non-fiction

Read the text and answer ALL the questions which follow.

The Amazon rainforest

The Amazon rainforest is the world's biggest tropical rainforest – as well as being the world's largest river basin. You'll probably have heard some shocking facts about how much of the Amazon forest is being cut down – the latest figures say the size of *three football pitches is disappearing per minute*. But amazingly, more than three quarters of the Amazon is still intact. So we want to focus on how we're helping to save what's left of this vast and vital natural treasure-trove, and what you can do to help. There is no time to lose; we need to get our skates on.

A healthy Amazon is clearly a good thing:

* Good for wildlife – half of all species on Earth are found in tropical rainforests. The Amazon contains a third of those forests. And it's likely there are lots more species still to be found there.

* Good for people – it has a vast store of valuable natural resources.

So it's obvious everyone should be protecting the Amazon, right?
We've found the best way forward is to work closely with local communities, governments and industry to create smart solutions that help both people and nature thrive in the Amazon.

We're determined to help protect large enough areas of the Amazon forests to save most of the animals that live there, and see that it can grow for the benefit of everyone.
And you can help right now... you can help us save this precious forest for future generations.

* Ask your parents to buy foods – like bananas and coffee – that are grown in a sustainable way. This is in a way that is safe for the environment, for wildlife, and for people. Buy Brazil nuts!

* Use sunflower oil, not palm oil, wherever possible.

* Ask your school to buy environmentally-friendly paper and recycle as much paper as you can.

* Tell your friends and family about how important the rainforests are, or ask your teacher to teach your class more about rainforests.

Adapted from WWF (World Wildlife Fund) www.wwf.org

1 Why has this text been written?											(1)
   a To give information about the WWF.
   b To advertise the WWF.
   c To persuade the reader to get involved.
   d To give instructions on how to cut down trees.

2 Give a synonym for each of these words from the text.						(3)
   a shocking   b vital   c create   d save   e large

3 Underline the words in this sentence which tell you that some progress has been			(1)
   made in the efforts to save the rainforest.

   We've found the best way forward is to work closely with local communities,
   governments and industry to create smart solutions that help both people and
   nature thrive in the Amazon.

4 Which words are used in the extract to show who is being asked to support the			(1)
   work of the WWF?

5 Add one of these suffixes to each of the words below to make a new word.			(3)

   | -ing   -ly   -able   -ful   –ment   -age |

   a large   b shock   c amaze   d help   e sustain

6 Punctuate these sentences properly by adding an apostrophe to show where			(2)
   letters have been missed out.
   a Its very important that the rainforest is saved.
   b If too many trees are cut down the animals wont have enough space to live.
   c The WWF havent stopped their work in other areas where animals are endangered.

7 Turn these words into plurals.									(3)
   a One government – two _____   b One community – two _____
   c One industry – two _____   d One generation – two _____

8 Underline the adverb in this sentence.								(1)
   But amazingly, more than three quarters of the Amazon is still intact.

9 Explain in your own words what this phrase means: *There is no time to lose;*			(1)
   we need to get our skates on.

10 Write a speech to give to your class about the things you could do to help			(4)
   save the Amazon rainforest. Remember to explain why it is important and think
   about ways in which you could all use less paper. Use persuasive words and
   phrases and think about how you will address your audience.

Recounting experiences

Cause and effect

> I can explore texts which tell about other people's experiences.

> I can write from more than one viewpoint.

1 Imagine you are the character in the picture. Write a diary entry about what happened on the beach that day.
Use these to help you:

| **Setting** | Where?
When? |

| **Character** | How were you feeling?
Who are you?
Give an interesting fact about yourself.
Remember to use nouns, verbs and adjectives. |

| **Events** | Think about cause and effect.
For example:
Cause: I did not wear a jacket when it rained.
Effect: I felt cold. |

Helpful hints

Flotsam is found on the beach. It is the word given to anything that has been washed ashore after being in the sea. In the story *Flotsam* by David Weisner, a young boy goes to the beach to search for flotsam.

Telling stories

> I can map out a story structure.

> I can create comparatives and superlatives.

Talk Partners

Talk with your partner about the character you have created and the diary entry you have written for him. Together make up a diary entry from the point of view of the person who lost the camera. How did they feel about losing it? What were they doing at the time? What events are in the lost photographs?

1 Draw and number six boxes like the ones opposite. Draw the new character's story in the boxes.

1	2	3
4	5	6

Talk Partners

Swap your drawings with your partner and tell each other's stories. Can you suggest ways the story could be improved?

2 Write a correct comparative or superlative for each of these sentences:

a The boys shouted loudly but the girls shouted the _____.

b On Monday the wind blew hard but on Tuesday it blew even _____.

c To come third the runner must be fast. To get first place the runner must be the _____.

d The garden plant had pretty flowers on it, however the plant in the house had _____ flowers.

e After a busy day at school the children were hungry but because Manika had not eaten any breakfast she was the _____.

Helpful hints

Words change when we use them to **compare** things. For example:
The old house was **big**. When we compare two houses we say: The old house was big but the new house is **bigger.**
It is also possible to say: The old house was big but the new house is the **biggest.**
The word **bigger** is a comparative to the word big, the word **biggest** is a superlative.

Muddled text

 1 The text below has become muddled – it is no longer in the right order. Write the letters of the paragraphs in the correct order.

a Howard Carter has become the most famous archaeologist in the world following his discovery of the tomb of Tutankhamun in 1922.

b The real hero of the discovery was actually a young water boy and not Carter at all.

c His stick made contact with something hard beneath the soft sand. When he brushed the sand away a stone step was revealed.

d There had been many rumours of a royal tomb in the area. Carter had been sponsored to find it though the money was beginning to run out.

e The water boy had fetched water for everyone and was taking a short rest. He had a stick he was pushing into the sand.

f He ran to fetch Carter who quickly started digging. He found a flight of steps which led down to a small, blocked up, stone door.

g The boy was working with Carter's team of archaeologists as they searched among the rock and sand for any clues which would lead them to the tomb.

> **Did you know?**
> Howard Carter was the British archaeologist who led the team which discovered Tutankhamun's tomb in 1922.

Talk Partners

Compare the order you have put the sentences into with your partner. Are there any differences? Is it possible to have some of the sections in a different order?
Can you spot any examples of cause and effect?

2 In these sentences which is the cause and which is the effect? For example: When the wind blew hard (cause) the man fastened his coat and held on to his hat (effect).

a The grass grew very quickly (_____) in the warmer weather (_____) .

b The cakes burnt (_____) when the oven temperature was too high (_____) .

c Nobody heard the telephone ring (_____) because the television was too loud (_____) .

d The unexpected shower of rain (_____) soaked the children (_____) as they walked home from school.

Prefixes

1 un-   im-   in-

Add one of the three prefixes above to these root words so they mean the opposite.

> usual   polite   even   correct

Helpful hints

A **prefix** is put in front of a root word to make another word. Sometimes the prefix makes the root word mean the opposite of what it meant originally. For example, the root word **possible** can mean the opposite by adding the prefix **im-**. The word becomes **impossible**.

2 Put the correct word that you have created in activity 1 into each of these sentences.

a   The alarm had a very _____ sound.
b   The _____ child was sent to bed early.
c   The answers to the maths problems were all _____ and had to be done again.
d   It was difficult to walk along the _____ path.

3 a   Tell the story of how the water boy (on page 53) found the steps to Tutankhamun's tomb from his point of view. Remember to include the key parts of the story. Begin like this:
I had just given everyone a drink …
b   Now tell the story from Howard Carter's point of view. Begin like this:
I heard the water boy calling me …

4 When we recount an event we often include how the character is feeling. The two characters in this recount are Howard Carter and the water boy. Copy and complete the table opposite, putting a tick on each line to show how each character felt when the steps were uncovered.

Feeling	Howard Carter	Water boy
proud		
relieved		
excited		
humble		
joyful		

Talk Partners

Talk with your partner about why you selected the character for these feelings. Use evidence from the text if you can.

Biography

Michael Morpurgo

Born: St Albans 1943

Previous jobs: Soldier and teacher

Michael Morpurgo lives in Devon with his wife Clare. He writes his books from home and helps Clare to run Farms for City Children, a project that takes children from inner-city schools to the countryside where they are given hands-on experience of what happens on a farm.

Michael has written over 100 books – all different, all exciting – and he draws on a lot of his own experience. He was sent away to boarding school, which he hated because he was homesick and because there was no privacy, and these are experiences that he draws on in *The Butterfly Lion* and *The War of Jenkins' Ear*. He enjoys writing. He didn't work especially hard at school but he was very good at games and this helped him to keep out of trouble.

When Michael left school he went into the army, which he also hated. He left as soon as he could and trained to be a teacher. Michael loved teaching, especially poetry, which he discovered through the poems of Ted Hughes.

He stopped teaching to become a full-time writer when he started the farm. He writes sitting up in bed with a thin pencil on lined paper which he fills as much as possible as he hates turning over and starting a new page!

Fact File

Michael Morpurgo
Born on October 5th 1943 in St Albans, UK.
Has written over 100 books.
Set up Farms for City Children project with wife, Clare.
Has three children.
Awarded an M.B.E. in 1999.
Awarded an O.B.E. in 2006.

Helpful hints

A **biography** is the story of someone's life and experiences.

A **fact file** merely lists facts about a person.

Talk Partners The two texts above have some similar information. Can you find three details which are in both texts? Talk about them and provide the evidence from each text to support what you have identified.

Did you know? The M.B.E. is a medal awarded to people who provide services for others. The O.B.E. is a medal awarded to people who have become well known nationally for work in their chosen area.

1 Copy and complete this table.

How Michael feels about these events	Positive	Negative	Don't know
born in St Albans			
went to boarding school			
was a soldier			
has three children			
awarded the O.B.E.			
lives in Devon			
writes books for children			

2 Provide evidence from the text on page 55 which shows how Michael Morpurgo feels about writing books.

3 Use a subordinating connective to join these sentences together.

a   It was warm and sunny in the morning _____ in the afternoon it turned much colder.

b   The children wore waterproof coats _____ the weather was forecast to be warm and sunny.

c   The sea was calm _____ it had been windy all morning.

d   The birds still came into the garden _____ the large cat sitting on the shed roof.

e   The children were still tired when they woke up _____ they went to bed early.

Helpful hints

When we want to write about two things which contrast in one sentence we can use a **subordinating connective**. For example: Michael Morpurgo finds writing exciting **however** he hates turning the page of his notebook so he writes as much as he can on one page. Subordinating connectives to show contrast include: although, even though, whereas, but, while, nevertheless, however, despite the fact.

Talk Partners

In Michael Morpurgo's biography the writer has used the words 'hated' and 'loved'. With your partner discuss how different words could be used which mean the same thing but give more impact.

Changes

In the extracts below we hear about some of the changes that have taken place in a small seaside village since World War Two broke out. The writer is an old lady, named Lily Tregenza, who is recounting events which happened when she was a 12-year-old girl.

The thing is Dad didn't need to go to fight the war; he could have stayed with us and helped Grandfather and Mum on the farm. Other farmers were allowed to stay. He could have. But he didn't.

We were sitting doing arithmetic when we heard the roaring and rumbling of an aeroplane, getting louder and louder, and the classroom windows started to rattle. Then there was this huge explosion and the whole school shook. We all got down on the floor and crawled under the desks like we have to do in air-raid practice, except this was much more exciting.

I'm fed up with this war. We're not allowed down on the beach any more to fly our kites. There's barbed wire all around it to keep us off, and there's mines buried all over it. They've put horrible signs up everywhere warning us off.

There was a massive hole in Mr Berry's cornfield just outside the village. No one had been hurt except a poor old pigeon who had been having a good feed of corn when the bomb fell.

Talk Partners

Read the extracts above. Lily tells the reader that her father did not need to go to fight the war. Talk about the decision he made and how he would have told his family. Think of the people he must tell – Grandfather, Mum and Lily. Work together to write what Dad would have said. Each take on the part of one of the other characters and reply to Dad. Think about how they would be feeling and what they would say to him.

Helpful hints

The bomb landed in Mr Berry's cornfield. An **apostrophe** has been used here to show that the cornfield belonged to Mr Berry. This is a **possessive apostrophe**.

1 Rewrite the sentences below with the possessive apostrophes in place.
   a   The farmers field was full of corn at harvest time.
   b   The childrens kites flew high in the sky.
   c   The womans hat blew across the road.
   d   It is everyones beach to play on.
   e   Where is Indys house?

Apostrophes

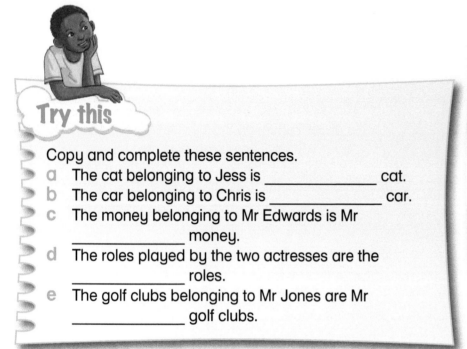

Try this

Copy and complete these sentences.

a The cat belonging to Jess is _____ cat.

b The car belonging to Chris is _____ car.

c The money belonging to Mr Edwards is Mr _____ money.

d The roles played by the two actresses are the _____ roles.

e The golf clubs belonging to Mr Jones are Mr _____ golf clubs.

Helpful hints

Using a **possessive apostrophe** with a word that ends in the letter **s** is tricky. For example, sometimes when someone's name ends in an 's' (like James) we write James's pen. But on other occasions (like Mr Hastings) we just add the apostrophe (Mr Hastings' pen). The best thing to do is say it out loud and work out which sounds right.

1 Copy and complete the table to show if the apostrophe has been used for possession or omission. Look back at the Helpful hints box on page 6 if you need to.

Word	possession	omission
the plants's roots		
don't		
he won't		
they shan't		
newspaper's readers		

2 Add a possessive pronoun to these sentences. Remember the object must belong to the subject of the sentence.

a The girl read _____ book.

b The drivers raced _____ cars around the track.

c It is nearly time for me to have _____ dinner.

d We must remember to take _____ tickets for the concert.

e Mira collected _____ shoes from the menders.

Helpful hints

Another way of showing that something belongs to someone (possession) is to use a **possessive pronoun**. For example: *The children ate their apples.* The apples (the object) belong to the children (the subject).

Moving times

The families of Slapton are all evacuated for a year so that the army can use the beach to practise on. These extracts are from Lily's diary as the family move in with Uncle George.

—————————————————————————— **Monday December 27th 1943**

It's my very last night in my own bedroom. Until now I don't think I thought it would ever really happen, not to us, not to me. It was happening to everyone else. Everyone else was moving out, but somehow I just didn't imagine that the day would ever come when we'd have to do the same. But tomorrow is the final day and tomorrow will come... I've never slept anywhere else in my whole life except in this room. For the first time I think I understand why Grandfather was being stubborn and difficult and grumpy. He loves this place, and so do I. I look around this room and it's a part of me. I belong here. I'll start to cry if I write any more, so I'll stop.

—————————————————————————— **Tuesday December 28th 1943**

Our first night at Uncle George's, and it's cold. But there's something worse than that, much worse. Tips has gone missing. We haven't got her with us.
We moved up here today. We were the last ones in the whole village to move out. Grandfather was very proud of that. We had lots of help...
I miss my room at home already. My bedroom here is not just cold, it's very small, a bit like a cupboard – a cupboard I have to share with Mum...
I wish Tips was here. I miss her and I'm really worried about her. She ran off when everyone came to the house to carry the furniture out. I called and called, but she didn't come.

—————————————————————————— **Thursday December 30th 1943**

I still can't find Tips. I've been looking for her all day today – and all day yesterday too.... Be there tomorrow, Tips. Please be there. It's your last chance.

Extracts from The Amazing Story of Adolphus Tips *by Michael Morpurgo*

Talk Partners

Read the extracts above. How can you tell that Lily is writing in her diary? Write down three pieces of evidence which you and your partner have found.

 Write your own reading log based on what you have read so far. Remember to include the main events, whether you would recommend this book and how it made you feel as you read it.

Taking on a role

Talk Partners

The families in *The Amazing Story of Adolphus Tips* were all ordered to leave their homes. Grandfather was not going to leave but he was persuaded to by the local school teacher whose husband had not returned from fighting with the British army abroad.

With your talk partner each take on the role of either Grandfather or the local school teacher. Think about what you would say to each other – present your own point of view and listen carefully to what the other person says.

Write down the conversation you have like this:

Grandfather:

School teacher:

Grandfather:

And so on – remember to answer each other's points and to give your own.

Present this to the rest of the class.

1 In *The Amazing Story of Adolphus Tips*, Lily has just one day to find her cat Tips before she can no longer go back to the house. Write the diary entry of her final search using adverbs at the start of each paragraph to link your writing, for example, *firstly, eventually, suddenly, quickly, finally* and *lastly*. Remember that paragraphs in diary entries are usually quite short.

2 Put commas into each of these sentences to make the reader pause and them easier to read.

   a   They went searching down in the bluebell wood down in the quarry.

   b   I could hear them all over the farm banging tins trying to call her trying to sweeten Tips in.

   c   They closed the barbed wire behind us then cutting us off from our home and from Tips.

   d   If they don't find her I'm going to crawl in under the wire and find her for myself no matter what they say.

Helpful hints

We use adverbs to give more information about the verb. An adverb can tell us about time, place or manner. We can use them to link our writing across paragraphs.

For example:

Eventually all of our belongings were at Uncle George's house.

Finally the animals were all settled in the barn.

Quickly I ran to open the barn door.

Comprehension

Lily continues to write her diary over the next year. She squeezes through the wire to go back to their old house to put food out for Tips until she realises another animal is eating it. Two American soldiers, Harry and Adie (short for Adolphus), befriend the children and visit the farm with special treats. Dad comes home on leave for a few days. Tips is found and returned to Lily by the Americans but has just had kittens and escapes as soon as she can to look after them. Finally the day comes when the family can move back home. To Lily's delight, Tips now returns home as well.

Extracts:

I should be happy but I'm not. This house isn't my home. It's an empty shell stacked with furniture, tea-chests everywhere, and it's damp.

The wallpaper's falling off above the chimney in the sitting room, and half a dozen of the windows are broken.

The gutters are full of grass and one drainpipe has fallen down into the garden and smashed the greenhouse.

I noticed some writing on the wall by the window, in pencil. This is what it says: January 10th 1944. Harry and Adie were here looking for Tips.

Supreme! Supreme! I feel supreme all over because just about the best thing that could happen has just happened, and it happened at breakfast time.

So all I've done today is cuddle Tips. I've decided that from now on she is always going to be called Adolphus Tips.

Extracts from The Amazing Story of Adolphus Tips *by Michael Morpurgo*

1 Read the extracts above. Copy this table and put a tick in the correct column to show how you expected Lily to feel and how she actually felt when she first saw the farm.

Feeling:	Happy	Unhappy	Excited	Upset	Pleased	Disappointed
How she felt						
How I expected her to feel						

2 You have looked at words which can be made into opposites of each other. When Lily found the message from Harry and Adie she was excited and pleased. Before she found the message she was unexcited and displeased.
Add the correct prefix to the words in bold to create the opposite: im- dis- mis- in-

a The _____ child was taught good manners and became **respectful.**

b Manto **spelt** nine words correctly in his spelling test but the last one was _____.

c The class did not **complete** the experiment so have to record the results as _____.

d The _____ water was made **pure** by boiling it.

Homophones

1 Copy the table below and write a short or one word sentence to describe these events from the synopsis on page 61.

Event	Short sentence
Tips escaped through the open kitchen door.	
Dad comes home on leave.	
The soldiers bring chocolate and hot dogs.	
The family move back home.	

Helpful hints

Michael Morpurgo has used very **short, one word sentences** to show how different characters react. For example: 'Supreme.' This describes how Lily feels when Tips walks into the house.

The story of Adolphus Tips was written for 'Boowie' – Lily's grandson. She fetched her diaries out of the loft and put the manuscript together before she flew to America. The story ends in the present.

So I went, Boowie, and that's where I am now, in Atlanta, in America. I don't think the two of us have stopped talking since the day I arrived – we have a lot of time to make up. And so when Adie asked me a week ago now, it seemed like the most natural thing in the world to say yes. We got married last Tuesday.

Extracts from The Amazing Story of Adolphus Tips *by Michael Morpurgo*

2 Read the extract above. Continue your reading log from page 59. Remember to include the main events from the story. Finish with a review of the book. What would you recommend about it and who would you recommend it to? Which was your favourite part? Is there anything about it you didn't like?

Helpful hints

Homophones are words which sound the same but are spelt differently and have different meanings. For example: I can **hear** the music if you put the radio **here**.

3 Underline the homophones in these sentences.
  a Two children are coming to the party.
  b We are not allowed to speak aloud during quiet time.
  c He threw the ball through the hoop.
  d They can wear their new shoes where they want to.
  e Please write on the right side of the page.

First person recounts

This extract is from a book about a fictional character called Tom Gates, who is in Year 5 at Oakfield School. He jokes and doodles his way through lots of hilarious situations.

Even though I only live four minutes away from school, I'm often late.

This is usually because me and Derek (my best mate and next-door neighbour) "chat" a bit (OK, a LOT) on the way. Sometimes it's because we get distracted by delicious fruit chews and caramel wafers at the shop. Occasionally, it's because I've had loads of other very important things to do.

For instance, this is what I did this morning (my first day back at school).

Woke up – listened to music

Played my guitar

Rolled out of bed (slowly)

Looked for socks

Looked for clothes

Played some more guitar

Realised I hadn't done my "holiday reading homework"

PANICKED – thought of good excuse for lack of homework (phew!).

Annoyed my sister, Delia. Which I must admit did take up a very LARGE chunk of the morning (time well spent though).

Hid Delia's sunglasses.

Took my comic into the bathroom to read (while Delia waited outside – Ha! Ha!).

When Mum shouts ... "Tom! You're LATE For School!"

Extract from The Brilliant World of Tom Gates *by Liz Pichon*

1 Read the extract above. Imagine you are Delia, writing about the same morning as Tom. Refer to Tom and the things he does to annoy you.

Talk Partners

Talk with a partner about Tom. What can you tell about his personality from this extract? Write down as much about him as you can.

Synonyms

I can collect synonyms and opposites.

1 Find synonyms for these words:
 a windless   b shiny
 c imagine   d eat
 e broken
For each pair of words write a sentence where both words would have the same meaning. For example:
It was a hot evening. It was a warm evening.

2 Find antonyms for these words:
 a true   b noisy
 c finish   d tidy
 e slow
Write a sentence for each word and its antonym.
For example: *The bag was heavy. The bag was light.*

3 Copy and complete this table.

Word	Synonym	Antonym
shout		
smooth		
tired		
joyful		
sharp		

4 Write more words after the given words which show degrees of meaning.
 a cross → angry →
 b shut → banged →
 c warm → hot →
 d tearful → sobbing →
 e cold → icy →

Helpful hints

A **synonym** is a word which means the same as another word. For example: *Tom* **admitted** *that teasing Delia took up a lot of time. Tom* **confessed** *that teasing Delia took up a lot of time.*

Admitted and **confessed** mean the same thing in this context.

When two words mean the opposite of each other this is known as an **antonym**. For example:
* The door was **open**. The door was **shut**.

Words can have degrees of meaning.
* The house was **large**.
* The house was **big**.
* The house was **enormous**.

The words large, big and enormous have degrees of meaning.

Using words for effect

Mr Fullerman (my form teacher) makes the whole class stand outside our room. He says

"Welcome BACK, Class 5F. I've got a BIG

surprise for you ALL."

(which is not good news.)

OH NO! He's rearranged ALL the desks! I'm now sitting right at the front of the class.

Worse still, Marcus "Moany" Meldrew is next to me.

This is a DISASTER. How am I going to draw my pictures and read my comics?

Sitting at the back of the class I could avoid the teacher's glares.

I am SO close to Mr Fullerman now I can see up his nose...

And if that's not bad enough, Marcus Meldrew IS the most annoying boy in the

WHOLE school. He is SO nosy and thinks he knows everything.

Extract from The Brilliant World of Tom Gates *by Liz Pichon*

 1 Read the extract above. Write a synonym for each of these words that appear in the extract.

whole   back   close   bad   annoying

 2 You started a reading log for *The Amazing Story of Adolphus Tips.* Now start a reading log for *The Brilliant World of Tom Gates.* What is your impression of the book so far?

Talk Partners

The Amazing Story of Adolphus Tips and *The Brilliant World of Tom Gates* are both written from the viewpoint of the main character but they are written very differently. Talk with your partner about the main differences.

Draw a diagram like this and put the things that are the same in the overlapping section and the particular features for each text in the separate sections.

The Brilliant World of Tom Gates   both   *The Amazing Story of Adolphus Tips*

Conversations

Mum and Dad are told that Tom has to stay behind after school because he drew a silly cartoon of his art teacher Mrs Worthington.

Dad gives me one of his little and tells me if I don't work hard at school, I'll end up like him. Not such a bad thing if you ask me, because Dad's got a pretty good job.

He has his own office (well it's a shed in our garden) where he works on his computer designing stuff. Occasionally he gets to work in other people's offices. Mum likes it when that happens because he has to look smarter and earns more money.

 I prefer it when Dad works at home because he has a SECRET stash of caramel wafers in the shed that I eat (and Mum doesn't know about).

Extract from The Brilliant World of Tom Gates *by Liz Pichon*

Talk Partners

Read the extract above. Dad talks to Tom about his detention and how the family feel about what he did. Write the conversation they have as dialogue.
Dad:
Tom:
Perform this for your class.

Try this

Write four sentences, using comparatives and superlatives (words that end in **–er** and **–est**) to explain to Tom why it is important to work hard in school. For example:
Children who work hard get **better** results in their examinations.
Parents are **proudest** when their children receive excellent reports.

What have I learnt?

Check what you have learnt in this unit:
* I know how to recognise a text which is about events. I can tell the difference between a diary and a biography.
* I can use comparative words, shades of meaning and opposites in my writing.
* I know how to see things from different points of view and can present my own viewpoint consistently when I speak and when I write.
* I can keep a reading log and use it to advise others about books I have read.

Myths, fables and legends

King Midas

The story of King Midas is a myth set in Ancient Greece.

The visitor

King Midas was a very rich man. He lived in a castle with his daughter Philomena. Philomena was a very beautiful girl with a smile that made everyone happy. King Midas loved Philomena dearly.

One day Philomena went to King Midas and said, "Father there's a stranger at our gates." King Midas sent a servant to see who the visitor was.

"My lord, it is Silenus, friend of the god Dionysus," reported the servant.

"Invite him in immediately, arrange for a lavish feast and the best entertainment. Prepare the best room for him," Midas ordered.

Midas and Silenus had much to talk about and the two men enjoyed many days in each other's company. But, all too soon it was time for Silenus to leave.

The god Dionysus was very grateful that Midas had been so helpful. "Midas, thank you for looking after Silenus. I would like to reward you," he said. "I will grant you any wish you make."

"Thank you," uttered Midas. "Please can I have some time to think so that I may wish carefully and wisely?" he asked.

King Midas was, after all, a rich man who had everything he needed. He spent a sleepless night, tossing and turning in his huge bed. In the morning he spoke to Dionysus and explained his greatest wish.

"I would like everything I touch to turn to gold," he said, proud of his clever idea. Surely this would make him the richest man on earth!

"Midas, are you sure that you have thought about this carefully," warned Dionysus. "Things may not turn out how you think!"

Talk Partners

Wishes are offered as a reward or present in many traditional tales. King Midas took a long time to think about his wish. With your partner talk about what you think he may have thought about but discarded. Copy and complete this table to help you.

Wish	Why discarded
A box full of gold	It will all be spent and there will be nothing left.

Writing a play

1 Read the story on page 67. In this story the characters speak to each other. For example: 'warned Dionysus'. In these sentences put in the word which shows how the character speaks.

  a   "Go and see who is at the palace gates," _____ Midas.

  b   "Yes, my lord," _____ the servant.

  c   "Order the cooks to prepare the finest banquet," _____ Midas.

  d   "I must leave in the morning," _____ Silenus.

  e   "Surely you can stay a little longer," _____ Midas.

2 Write a list of all the characters who speak in the extract on page 67.

3 Write a play, including speech and stage directions for the section of the extract where Midas and Dionysus talk about the wish. Think about where this will take place and what is said.

Talk Partners

Share your play with your partner. Look at the things which you have done differently and things you have done in the same way. Use both of your ideas to make one play. Perform it for the class.

Helpful hints

In this extract from the myth there are **characters** – people who are included in the story. The **setting**, where everything takes place, is the palace of King Midas.

A **play** is written very differently to a story. The actors must know what to say (their lines) and what to do (stage directions). It is important to make it clear which is which when you write a play. For example:

Setting: the courtyard of King Midas's palace. King Midas is sitting on a throne being fanned by a servant.

(Philomena enters.)

Philomena: Father, there is a stranger at our gate. He is asking for you.

Midas: Servant, go immediately to the gate and see who it is.

Servant: Yes, your majesty.

(Servant puts down the fan and leaves the courtyard.)

When we are ordering numbers we sometimes use the letter string **nth**. For example: The **ninth** letter in the alphabet is **i**.

4 Match the **nth** words to each of these definitions.

                                           umpteenth tenth month seventh

  a   February is the second one in the year.

  b   Coming one after sixth.

  c   An unspecified large number.

  d   Each of ten equal parts.

Identifying a myth

Be careful what you wish for

"Starting tomorrow morning, with the first of the sun's rays, you will get the golden touch," promised Dionysus.

King Midas thought he must be dreaming – this couldn't be true. But the next day when he woke up he touched the bed, his clothes and everything turned to gold! He was delighted! So many riches, and they were all his!

Midas was hungry. "Fetch me fruit," he called to a passing servant. "And a large jug of water to quench my thirst," Midas added.

The servant returned with a juicy peach, on a silver platter, and a jug filled with cold, clear water. He set it down carefully in front of Midas. Midas put the peach to his lips and bit into solid gold, he raised the pitcher to his mouth and the water turned solid before it touched his lips.

He walked out into the courtyard feeling very pleased with himself. Philomena came running towards him and he hugged her. She turned into a gold statue. There were no more smiles left.

The king bowed his head and started crying.

Did you know?

In myths the gods and goddesses talk with the human characters. The gods and goddesses can make extraordinary things happen. There is often a lesson, or a moral, to be learnt from the story.

1 Read the extract above. Which of these sections from the text tell you that this is a myth?
   a "Starting tomorrow morning with the first of the sun's rays you will get the golden touch," promised Dionysus.
   b But the next day when he woke up, he touched the bed, his clothes, and everything turned to gold.
   c The servant returned with a juicy peach, on a silver platter, and a jug filled with cold, clear water.
   d Midas put the peach to his lips and bit into solid gold.
   e The king bowed his head and started crying.

Helpful hints

The king has many different aspects to his **character**. For example, he is kind and generous to a visitor. Silenus is greeted and given food, he is entertained and given a room for the night.

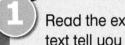

Talk Partners

With your partner talk about the different characteristics King Midas shows in the myth. Support your views of him with evidence. Copy and complete this table to help you.

Characteristic	Evidence
Kind and generous	Welcomes a visitor, providing food, entertainment and shelter

Philomena's story

I can write a story from another viewpoint.

I can spell words which have suffixes added which begin with a vowel.

1 We know about Midas's character because of the way he acts and the way he reacts to different characters in the myth. Can you write the myth from Philomena's point of view, starting with the arrival of the visitor? Remember to include details which tell us about King Midas. Begin like this:
I rushed to tell my father a visitor was asking for him at the gate.
Finish at the point where Philomena sees her father standing in the courtyard and runs to hug him.

2 a Add one of these suffixes to each of the root words in the cloud:
-ed   -ing   -able   -ish

> organise   like   love   age
> rogue   humble   write

b Now put each word in a grammatically correct sentence.

Helpful hints

Some words end in a silent **e**. For example: drive, lame, use. When we add a suffix which begins with a vowel to these root words the silent **e** is removed. For example: root word **drive** plus suffix **-able** becomes **drivable**. The car was **drivable**.

Talk Partners

Talk about how King Midas feels now that Philomena has been turned to gold. Write down as many words as you can which explain how he feels. Talk about what he should do next. Are there any ways in which he can get his beloved daughter back? Choose one idea from those you have discussed and write a plan to make it happen.

Try this

How many new words can you make by combining the suffixes and root words from activity 2?

Animal characteristics

A lesson learnt

King Midas did not know what to do. He was hungry. He was thirsty. The most precious part of his life was lost to him. He had barked up the wrong tree.

"If only I had not been so greedy!" he shouted. Dionysus could see that the king was the most miserable man. He asked, "What would you rather have, your loving and most precious daughter or untold wealth?" The king cried out for forgiveness, "I will give up all my gold if I could just have my daughter back. Without her I have lost everything worth having."

Dionysus smiled and said to the king, "You have become wiser," and he reversed the wish. Midas got his daughter back in his arms, he had learnt a lesson that he would never forget. He was on top of the world.

Did you know?

There are many different versions of this myth. In one version Dionysus insists that King Midas wear a pair of donkey ears for the rest of his life.

Talk Partners

Read the text above. Talk with your partner about what wearing donkey ears would symbolise? How would Midas feel? Would he actually need to wear donkey ears to feel this way? Can you think of any other animal characteristics we use to show how people act. Think about an animal you describe as cunning or proud. Make a list with your partner and then share it with the class.

Helpful hints

An **idiom** is a word or phrase which does not mean what it literally says but whose meaning is understood. For example: *I could eat a horse.* This shows that the person who said it is very hungry, but they could not literally eat a horse.

1 The writer has used idioms in this extract from the myth of King Midas. At the end of the myth he is 'on top of the world'. This means he is overjoyed.
Can you match the meaning with the correct idiom?

Idioms	Meanings
a To get into hot water	a To go on a useless search
b To spill the beans	b To tell a secret
c A wild goose chase	c To pretend to cry
d To live it up	d To get into trouble
e To shed crocodile tears	e To enjoy life

Poetry performance

This is an extract from a poem written about King Midas.

I can perform a narrative poem.

"To say thank you for being such a
Decent and honourable king,
I'm going to grant you one wish,
You can wish for anything."
The king was thrilled, and he replied,
"Well, thank you very much!
I would like to turn into gold
Everything that I touch."

Before too long King Midas saw
A beautiful purple flower.
He thought "This would be a good thing
On which to test my new power".

He touched a tree, a rock, a twig,
And they all transformed too.
The king could hardly believe it,
His great wish had really come true.

Feeling hungry, he got some food,
And put on the kettle.
But these things, of course, also turned
Into precious metal.

"Oh dear" he thought, "I think perhaps
I need a little rest."
He lay down on his bed but...well...
You've probably already guessed.

By Paul Perro

1 Read the poem. In it the king is shown as being very pleased with his wish. Can you find the words the author has used to show this? For example, 'thrilled'.

Talk Partners

With your partner add a verse to this poem. Remember to add the next stage of the story.

Talk Partners

Talk about how this narrative poem could be performed. Practise together, adding actions and expressions to the performance. Perhaps it could be performed by two people. How would you divide the poem for this to happen? Perform this (with any extra verses you have added) for the rest of the class.

Pandora's Box

The story of *Pandora's Box* is another myth set in Ancient Greece.

Once up a time, a long time ago, there were two brothers named Epimetheus and Prometheus. They were gods. They were kind.

Prometheus felt sorry for man who was happy when the warm sun smiled down on him but who complained to the gods as he shivered from the cold in winter. Prometheus stole fire from heaven and gave it to man. Zeus, the leader of the gods, was furious. He had announced that man did not deserve fire and Prometheus had ignored him. As punishment, Zeus chained Prometheus to a rock for many years.

Zeus ordered the gods' handyman, the maker of things – Hephaestus – to make him a daughter. Hephaestus made a woman out of clay and then breathed life into her. The gods all bestowed gifts upon her; beauty, speech, curiosity. Zeus named his lovely new daughter Pandora. She was the light of his life.

Zeus gave Pandora in marriage to the good-hearted Epimetheus. He presented the couple with a wedding gift. The present was a container with a locked lid and the key attached.

"Do not ever open this container," he warned.

Did you know?

This myth is often called *Pandora's Box* but many people say that at the time this story was set the container would have been a large jar.

---

1 Read the extract above. Which of these features of myths are in the text? Copy and complete the table. One has been done for you.

Feature	Present in this extract	Evidence
Usually set in the past		
Explain why the world is as it is		
Often include a quest or journey		
The gods and humans talk	yes	*The humans complained they were cold and Prometheus gave them fire.*
Supernatural things happen		

2 In the extract above there are two examples of metaphors. *The warm sun smiled down. She was the light of his life.* Turn these metaphors into similes.
  a   The shiny round coin of a pond.
  b   Smoke cottonwool balls billowing out of the chimney.
  c   Her stomach was a bottomless pit.
  d   The velvet tones of his singing soothed the crowd.
  e   Starry beacons shone down from the sky.

Questions

I can check subject-verb agreement in a sentence.

Helpful hints

This myth is used to give an explanation for something which has happened in the world.

You can guess what happened next. Pandora had been given curiosity as a gift from the gods. One day she could contain it no longer and she used the key to open the jar. As she raised the lid, out flew all the bad things contained inside it – including envy, sickness, hate and disease. Pandora slammed the lid closed, but it was too late, they were released into the world.

Epimetheus heard her weeping and he came running. Pandora opened the lid to show him the jar was empty.

One small thing had been left in the jar. Quickly, before she could slam the lid shut, it flew out. That thing was named Hope. And Hope made all the difference in the world.

Talk Partners

Read the extract above and with your partner talk about what is being explained in it. List the negative things which the jar may have contained – the things which make life uncomfortable and unhappy. Together write a poem about how *Hope* battles against these things. For example:

* disease, injury and pain – bringing misery to those who are ill
* hope – that cures may be found and people will get better.

Practise saying your poem in alternate lines.
Perform it for your class.

Helpful hints

Do you know when to use **I** and when to use **me**? It's easy. For example: Should it be – *The tickets were for my friends and I* or *The tickets were for my friends and me*? Simply take away the friends. So, you would not say *The tickets were for I*, you would say *The tickets were for me*. The answer therefore is *The tickets were for my friends and me.*

1 Choose **I** or **me** for these sentences.
 a   My mother and (I/me) went shopping last week.
 b   Dad and (I/me) won the race.
 c   Grandad took (I/me) in his car.
 d   He is better at maths than (I/me).
 e   The shoes fit my brother better than they fit (I/me).

The Ant and the Grasshopper

The story of *The Ant and the Grasshopper* is a Greek fable.

One summer's day, in a sunny field, a grasshopper was hopping about, chirping and singing to his heart's content. An ant passed by, struggling to carry an ear of corn he was taking to the nest.

"Come and play with me," said the grasshopper, "it's a lovely day. Why toil on such a sunny day when you could be having fun?"

"I am building up my stores for the winter when there will be nothing to eat," said the ant, "and it would be a good idea if you did the same."

"I am not worried about winter," replied grasshopper. "I have plenty to eat at present. Make hay while the sun shines I say."

The ant trundled on, carrying corn which weighed more than he did. Slowly the larder filled with seeds which would last him through the longest and coldest of winters.

The long, warm summer days slowly gave way to the sharp frosts and chilly nights of autumn. Then the snows came and winter settled its mantle over the countryside.

Aesop, adapted by Anne Basden

Helpful hints

A **fable** is a short story which often, but not always, has animals for characters. Fables have a moral – that is a message about the actions of the characters.

1 Read the extract above. Match the animal to the way it acts.

ant   grasshopper

lazy organised unprepared playful hard-working wise

Did you know?

Aesop was a famous fable teller in Greek times. He was a slave who earned his freedom by telling fables to entertain guests when his master had visitors for huge feasts.

2 Many of the words in this extract have had **–ing** added. Give the root word for each of these words:
a hopping   b singing   c taking
d chirping   e struggling f having

Talk Partners

Read the extract above again. The ant and the grasshopper have very different points of view. The grasshopper would like the ant to play. The ant would like the grasshopper to work. Prepare a dialogue where you each take on one of the characters' points of view. Do not argue – persuade!

Understanding the moral

The moral

Ant settled into his snug nest. He took grain and seeds from his store cupboard every day and waited for the spring to bring the warmth back to the earth.

Grasshopper had no food and found himself cold and miserable as winter wore on. He remembered the industrious ant who walked past him while he played in the warmth of the summer sun. He left his miserable home and knocked on ant's door.

"I am hungry," he said. "Please take pity on me. Spare some of the food you have in your stores to help me survive the winter cold."

Ant remembered the way grasshopper had mocked him as he worked through the summer days. He remembered grasshopper boasting that he did not need to prepare for winter.

"I have no food to spare," he replied. "I worked while you played and now I will reap the reward for my efforts." He shut the door and returned to his nest where he would stay, well fed, until the warmer weather returned.

Aesop, adapted by Anne Basden

> **Helpful hints**
>
> In **fables** the actions of animals are used to show humans how they should act and to highlight the consequences of making bad decisions.

1 Read the extract above. Which of these could be a suitable moral for the fable of the ant and the grasshopper?

   a Make hay while the sun shines.
   b Be not hasty to envy the condition of others.
   c Idleness brings want.
   d Friends will always provide.
   e Prepare today for the needs you have tomorrow.

> **Try this**
>
> *Can you write your own moral for this fable?*

2 Can you find the words in the text which mean the same as:
   a nice home
   b hard-working
   c teased
   d talked proudly
   e get something good

> **Helpful hints**
>
> The writer has used **well-chosen words** and **alliteration**, for example: *winter wore on* to help the reader remember the text.

Writing a fable

I can write my own fable.

The ant spent the long winter in his well-stocked nest. When the spring returned he hopped out to enjoy the first of the sun's rays.

 1 Use a pronoun in place of the underlined word in each sentence.

a   The boy's mother told <u>the boy</u> to go to bed.
b   The children were cold so <u>the children</u> put warm jumpers on.
c   The girl was late for school so <u>the girl</u> ran quickly.
d   The washing machine was broken so <u>the washing machine</u> needed repairing.
e   Jelilat and Samson are brother and sister so <u>Jelilat and Samson</u> have the same parents.

Helpful hints

We use **pronouns** to avoid repeating names when we write. For example: the ant/he/his.

Talk Partners

Think of a situation where the story of the ant and the grasshopper could be about two people. For example, the ant could be a learner who studies hard and completes all his or her homework. The grasshopper could be a learner who watches television and does not study. Which one will get good grades? Which will have to work hard to catch up? Talk together to think about situations that this could be applied to. Share these with the class.

Writing presentation

You are going to write your own fable.

First you need to think of the moral you would like to demonstrate. Think of a way that people act which could be improved such as laziness or greed. Can you think of the way an animal acts which naturally shows this? Give your fable a setting and think about using careful word choices and alliteration for effect.

Afterwards, check through your story and underline any words that are spelt incorrectly. Write these words in your spelling journal and practise spelling them correctly.

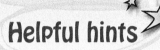

Did you know?

Aesop told many fables. The animals he used had many human characteristics such as being able to talk. They also kept the characteristics which humans knew them by. For example, the hare sprints fast and the tortoise plods along slowly in *The Hare and the Tortoise*.

Robin Hood

The legend of Robin Hood

The Sheriff of Nottingham had placed many rewards for the capture of Robin Hood but he always managed to escape. His 'Merry Men' always made sure that Robin knew whenever the sheriff had any new plan to catch him.

The rich were scared to travel through Sherwood Forest because they knew Robin Hood would attack. The poor were always pleased to see him.

Finally, the Sheriff thought of a brilliant plan. "Let's have a competition to see who is the best marksman in Nottingham. Robin Hood will not be able to resist such a competition. He will surely come. When he does, my guards will seize him," he explained. Everyone agreed that this was a splendid plan.

Now, Robin Hood was an excellent marksman; there was none better than him with a bow and arrow in the whole of Nottingham. Would Robin Hood be able to resist taking part in any competition to prove that he was the best?

Helpful hints

A legend is a story which has been passed on through many generations. It usually involves a heroic person. It is thought that there is some truth in legends, that they did actually occur though the events are not actually recorded in history.

Robin Hood was a legendary figure who lived in England about 700 years ago. He was an outlaw who stole money from the rich and gave it to the poor. He lived with a gang, known as the Merry Men, in Sherwood Forest, near Nottingham. In some pictures he is shown as having red hair and wearing a green outfit.

1 Read the extract above. Give a word which has the root word **guard** for each of these definitions.
  a   Someone who rescues swimmers.
  b   To make sure something is protected.
  c   Placed around a fire to protect it.

Talk Partners

With your partner discuss what makes Robin Hood a legendary figure.

2 The word **guard** can be used as a noun or a verb. Copy and complete the table below to show how it has been used in these sentences. Tick the correct box.

Sentence	Verb	Noun
He was sent to guard the prisoner.		
The guard was looking the other way when the prisoner escaped.		

Messages in words

The trap is set

Robin Hood summoned his loyal men by blowing his hunting horn. They all tried to stop him from competing. "Robin, this competition is being held to trap you," said Little John, a giant of a man who stood over six feet tall. "It would be foolish, you will be walking into the lion's den," said Will Scarlett, the youngest of the gang. But Robin Hood was not willing to listen.

The next day the crowds flocked to the competition. Ten contestants were there. The Sheriff asked, "Has my plan worked? Is Robin here?" "No, my lord. None of the contestants have red hair." The Sheriff said, "He must be scared."

The competition began. Slowly the competitors were eliminated until only two remained. One was the Sheriff's top guard, William. The other a dark haired young man dressed in green. They were both keen to win the first prize, a silver arrow. It was time for the last arrow to be shot; the winner of this round would be declared the best marksman in Nottingham.

Helpful hints

Sometimes writers use words to make a point more strongly. The words do not mean exactly what they say. This is called an **idiomatic phrase**.

1 Read the extract above. Will Scarlett warned Robin by saying "You will be walking into the lion's den." This was to show him how dangerous it would be to attend the competition. Match these idioms with their meanings:

Idioms	Meanings
a part of the furniture	a really heavy downpour
b deep pockets but short arms	b get your energy back
c raining cats and dogs	c always there
d recharge your battery	d solve a problem
e tackle an issue	e never pay for anything

Helpful hints

Remember how to spell words which have the letters **ie** in them: 'i before **e** except after **c**'. This rule is usually very helpful but only when the **ie** letters make the sound **ee**. So in the word **science** this rule does not apply.
Some words just do not follow the rule and it is important to learn these.

2 Choose which of these spellings in the words below follow the **ie** rule and which do not.

> chief   weird   receipt   seize
> thief   ceiling

Persuasion

I can write my own version of a legend.

I can use paragraphs.

Talk Partners

Read the text on page 79. Imagine you are two of Robin's 'merry men'. You know about the competition and Robin's plan to attend. How would you try to stop him going? Think about persuasive words you would use to do this.

In your pairs each take the part of Robin or the merry man who tries to stop him competing. Perform the conversation the two characters have for the rest of the class.

Helpful hints

A **paragraph** is used to group sentences together which are about the same topic. For example, if you are writing about your home you would use an introductory paragraph to explain where it is, then a paragraph to write about who lives there, another paragraph to write about inside the home and another paragraph to write about the outside.

The escape

William took aim first and shot; the arrow was very close to the centre of the target. The Sheriff applauded. "Good shot, William," he said. "The prize is in the bag." Then it was the turn of the man in green; he fired his arrow. The crowd cheered hysterically. It went through William's arrow and hit the bullseye.

Within a flash the man in green fired two more arrows which flew towards the chair on which the Sheriff was sitting and stuck on either side of it. The Sheriff was stunned.

The man in green was Robin Hood. Before the Sheriff could speak, Robin pulled off his black wig, threw it in the ground, jumped over a wall on to his waiting horse and was gone. "Get him, you fools. That is Robin Hood," shouted the helpless Sheriff, but it was too late. Robin Hood had escaped again.

1 Write your version of the competition from the viewpoint of one of the 'merry men'.
Remember to include the way in which the Sheriff of Nottingham acts and try to build up the excitement of the final round.
Use paragraphs to guide the reader through the story.

Can you find the idiom in the extract on this page?

Try this

A legend in a poem

The Ballad of Robin Hood

In days of old when the knights were bold
Lived a man called Robin Hood.
Who robbed the rich to feed the poor
He was valiant, brave and good.
When the Sheriff's men searched the forest glen,
There was nowhere could they find.
The fearless blade and his lovely maid,
There was neither hair nor hide

Rob roamed the glen with his merry men.
Giving substance to the poor.
Folk far and wide spoke his name with pride,
In the bygone days of yore.
In days of old when the knights were bold
Lived a man called Robin Hood.
Who robbed the rich to feed the poor
He was valiant, brave and good.

From The Robin Hood Musical

 1 Read the poem opposite. Find the words that the writer has used to show how he felt about Robin? For example: valiant (brave).

Talk Partners With your partner talk about what you know about Robin Hood from the poem. Write down a list and share it with the rest of the class. Ask questions about how you know and use evidence from the poem to support your findings.

 2 Copy and complete the table below. Tick the correct column to show which text (the poem or the story) tells you the information.

Information	Story	Poem
The Sheriff of Nottingham wanted to capture Robin		
The Sheriff of Nottingham's men searched for Robin		
Robin was an excellent marksman		
Robin disguised himself.		

 What have I learnt?

Check what you have learnt in this unit:
* I can identify the key features of a myth, a fable and a legend.
* I know what an idiomatic phrase is, why writers use them and I can work out what the writer means.
* I can write my own fable.
* I know some strategies to help me spell some unfamiliar words.

Unit 6 A longer story

North Child

This extract is written from the viewpoint of Neddy, one of the children in the family.

North Child is based on the Norwegian fairy tale *East of the Sun and West of the Moon*. The author, Edith Pattou, has won many awards for her work including Booklist Top Ten Fantasy Novel of the Year.

'Once upon a time there was a poor farmer with many children.'

It was during just such a storm-drenched night, as we huddled around the hearth, that we heard a scratching sound coming from our front door. Mother was at the far end of the great room, sitting by Sara, who had just fallen into a fitful sleep.

The sound came again, and after exchanging a look with Father I went to the door and cautiously opened it a crack, wondering who or what could be out on such a night.

All I saw was a white blur before the door was flung wide. I stepped back and something large and wet brushed past me.

I turned to stare at an enormous white bear standing in the middle of the great room.

The wind howled in, spewing cold rain, but we were unaware of it.

"Close the door." It was a massive, strange voice. And though it seemed impossible, I knew at once the voice was coming from the white bear.

My sister Sonja swayed and looked like she might faint. I moved to her quickly, putting an arm around her shoulders. She was trembling.

Rose went to the door and shut it.

It was like a dream, gazing at the immense animal that had entered our home. Standing erect on all four feet, he was as tall as me, and water dripped off him onto the wooden floor. And I remembered water dripping off fur from long ago.

I guessed from the moment he brushed by me that this was the white bear I had seen as a child, the one that had saved my sister Rose. If I had any doubts they were dispelled when I looked into those black eyes. It was the same bear. And I was filled with terrible foreboding.

From North Child *by Edith Pattou*

1 Read the extract above. The writer has used words which have prefixes in front of them (**im**possible, **un**aware). Write the two root words in a new sentence.

2 The writer uses the word 'dispelled'. This means to get rid of. A synonym (another word which means the same) for dispelled is banished. Copy and complete the table opposite, writing a synonym for each word.

Word	Synonym
middle	
flung	
immense	
terrible	
cold	

Reading log

I can predict what will happen next.

Talk Partners

In the extract on page 82 the writer describes the weather. She uses these phrases: 'storm-drenched night', 'The wind howled in, spewing cold rain'. Discuss with your partner what impression these give you of the weather outside. Can you think of another phrase you could add? Share your phrase with the rest of the class.

1 Copy and complete the table below, giving two phrases for each type of weather. One has been done for you.

Weather	Descriptive phrases
snowfall	the weight of the snow silenced our words blinding white flakes fluttered in the bitter cold air
heatwave	
foggy	
thunderstorm	
drizzle	

2 Many characters are mentioned in the extract on page 82. We can deduce something about them from what has been written.
Mother is sitting by Sara. Deduction: Mother is caring for Sara.
Sara has fallen into a fitful sleep. Deduction: Sara is unwell.
Sonja sways as if she might faint. Deduction: Sonja is frightened by the bear.
With a partner, write what the author tells you about these characters and make a deduction:
a Rose b Neddy c The bear

3 Start a reading log for *North Child*. Write two reasons why a reader would continue to read this book and predict what you think will happen next. Remember to refer to specific characters or events from the story to support your answers.

A new home

The bear makes a bargain with the family. He will make sure that Sara gets better and they will all do well if Rose goes with him. This extract is written from Rose's viewpoint.

When I awoke, my head was heavy. But I knew where I was right away. At home, even in summer, there would be a cold tang to the air in the morning and the mattress I slept on with my sister was not covered in velvet and overstuffed with down.

I sat up, stretching, and saw that the table had been cleared while I slept, except for a covered basket, a crock of butter beside it, and a large white teapot. Steam was rising from the pot's spout. My stomach growled and I realised I was ravenous again.

From North Child *by Edith Pattou*

1 Read the extract above. The writer has used two expressions which do not mean exactly what they say to describe how Rose feels. Can you find them and explain what they mean?

2 In the extract above there are two words which have the same letters but which are pronounced differently; 'raven**ous**' and 'sp**ou**t'. Write out the words in this box where the **ou** sounds the same as the **ou** in spout.

> sound   mysterious   ridiculous   house   south   marvellous

3 Write out the words in this box where the **ou** sounds the same as **ou** in ravenous.

> found   famous   sour   cousin
> rough   mysterious

Helpful hints

One of the ways we use commas is to separate information which is not essential to the meaning of the sentence. For example: Michael, who is 30 years old, is a very good goalkeeper. The extra information about Michael's age has been separated from the sentence by a pair of commas as it forms a subordinate clause.

4 Use a pair of commas to separate the additional information in these sentences.

a   The bonfire which was lit at seven o'clock was still burning the next morning.

b   Next Friday which happens to be my birthday is the day we are going on holiday.

c   The food on the other hand was delicious.

d   The garage mechanics who all live nearby could not repair the gear box.

A letter home

The white bear was really a man who was under the enchantment of the Troll Queen. Rose cannot contain her curiosity and she lights a candle so she can see his face. She spills candlewax on the shirt he is wearing. This strengthens the Troll Queen's enchantment and she takes him far away. Rose must find where he is being kept to rescue him.

Dear Neddy,

I am writing to tell you that I am safe and well and no longer living at the castle with the white bear. It is a long story and one I hope to tell you at the end of my journey. But I made a wrong choice, one that hurt someone very badly, so I must now undertake a journey to a far distant land – one that lies east of the sun and west of the moon.

Because you are cleverer than me, you will have already figured out that there is no such land. Nevertheless, I go there. It seems right somehow that I should journey to a place that does not exist; it is where Mother always feared I would end up.

And please tell Mother that the candle worked all too well. But tell her, too, that the choice to use it was mine and I do not blame her.

Just as the blame is mine, the journey, too, is mine and I must undertake it alone. So do not try to come to me. I need to set right the wrong I have done, and when I have I will return home. Trust me, Neddy, and try not to worry.

Your sister, Rose.

From North Child *by Edith Pattou*

Helpful hints

Pronouns are used in place of nouns in a sentence. They help us to write without repeating the noun. For example: <u>The car</u>'s owner washes <u>the car</u> every week. Replace 'the car' with the word 'it'. The car's owner washes it every week.

1 Read the letter above. In Rose's letter she uses pronouns to refer to Mother (her), Neddy (you) and herself (I). Replace the underlined nouns in these sentences with a pronoun that makes sense.

a The house needs a new coat of paint to help the owners sell <u>the house</u>.

b When Mother went to the shops <u>Mother</u> bought some flour so <u>Mother</u> could make a cake.

c Tell the children that the minibus is booked for <u>the children's</u> trip tomorrow.

d Peter wore new shoes to school, the field was muddy so <u>Peter's</u> new shoes got dirty.

e When the telephone rang the family were having tea so <u>the family</u> did not answer <u>the telephone.</u>

Talk Partners

In her letter, Rose tells Neddy to try not to worry. Talk with your partner about the things that would worry Neddy.

I can proofread and edit my own writing.

Writing a letter

Writing presentation

Read the letter on page 85 again. Write a letter back to Rose as if you were Neddy. Use any of the information you have from the story so far. Think carefully about the words you will use to tell Rose how you feel, but also the words you will use to support her on the journey.

Talk Partners

Read your letter aloud to your talk partner. Proofread your own letter and discuss any improvements you could each make. Think about how you have used connectives and how you have punctuated your sentences. Have you varied the length of your sentences? Rewrite your letters with the improvements included.

1 Fill in your reading log. Write two reasons why a reader would want to read the next part of the story. Remember to refer to specific characters or events from the story.

2 Copy the table and write the name of the character from the words they use. The characters are the white bear, Rose, Neddy and Mother.

Words spoken		Character
a	I had once told Rose that if she needed me I would go to her, no matter where she was.	
b	I … I gave them to Rose. The candle …. Oh, what have I done?	
c	The stories I read to him were good, especially when we would laugh at something funny. Though the sound of a white bear laughing out loud is not for the faint of heart.	
d	The one who lies near death will be made well again. And you will no longer be poor but wealthy, and will live in comfort and ease.	

A dangerous journey

Rose has to travel to a land east of the sun and west of the moon to rescue the white bear. On this part of her journey she gives one of her dresses in exchange for a place on a boat. A terrible storm blows up. The sailors are very frightened and they lower the sails to try to keep safe.

… and then there was a great violent crashing sound as a giant wave slammed down on the knorr.

When I came to, I could still hear the wind, but it was no longer screaming. Miraculously the ship was still afloat... I could hear no other sounds but the creaking of the ship, the sloshing of water around me and the diminishing fury of the wind.

Gingerly, my head pounding, I wriggled my body backwards, then slowly pulled myself out from under the deck boards. I sat up, waist-deep in water, and the ship seemed to spin dizzily for a few moments. I closed my eyes, then opened them.

I could see no one.

From North Child *by Edith Pattou*

Talk Partners

Read the extract above. Imagine yourself in Rose's place. With your talk partner write down how she must be feeling and what she is thinking.

Glossary

knorr: a large, flat bottomed boat which is driven by sail

1 The writer uses words to tell the reader about the storm.
   a   In the first sentence which words show how forceful the storm was?
   b   In the first sentence which word is used to show how big the wave was?
   c   Put these words in order to show how a wind can be described as getting stronger.

   | blustery | breezy | brisk | wild | screaming | whipping |

Talk Partners

Share with your partner the words you found in activity 1. Talk about why the writer chose these words and what effect they have on the reader.

2 Work out where the apostrophe should go in these sentences.
   a   Roses journey was long and dangerous.
   b   The ships crew put the sails down during the storm.
   c   Slowly the winds force died down and the waves became less violent.
   d   Rose wriggled backwards and pulled her legs out of the ships hold.

I can set out dialogue.

A different viewpoint

Every day the white bear man is given a special drink, called slank, by the Troll Queen. This makes him forget Rose and everything from his past. A wedding is arranged between him and the Troll Queen, who has given him the name Myk. Tuki, a servant, helps Rose.

Just before the wedding Rose reaches the Ice Palace and works as a servant. Every day she swaps Myk's potion with a plain drink.

On the day of the wedding Myk has a special request for the Troll Queen. He wants her to wash a piece of his clothing. The extract below is written from the Troll Queen's viewpoint.

"My Queen? Will you grant my request?"

The murmuring grew louder. My people knew this was out of the ordinary. They were waiting for my response. Myk's eyes were on me, too.

"Yes, Myk. I will honour this tradition of your land, and after I have done it, then we shall proceed." It was annoying but the proposition was a simple one. With my arts I could wash anything clean.

"Then you agree to honour my tradition – I shall marry the one who washes a garment of my choosing."

All eyes were on us. Tuki let out a little squeaking sound. His pathetic eyes shone with excitement. It was then I felt the first glimmer of unease. I did not see how Myk should have memories of wedding traditions of his homeland when he drank the slank every day. But I could not back down, not with my people watching. It would make me look weak.

From North Child *by Edith Pattou*

Helpful hints

Speech marks (sometimes called inverted commas) are used to punctuate speech. If the words are followed by how and who they were spoken by there must be a comma, question mark or exclamation mark before the closing speech marks. For example: "Please watch carefully when you cross the road," said Mum.

"Watch when you cross the road!" warned Mum.

"Did you watch when you crossed the road?" asked Mum.

Writing presentation

Read the extract above. Using dialogue (the words she speaks) continue this extract as the Troll Queen organises her washing of the shirt. Begin like this:

"Bring me water and soap," I ordered.

Afterwards, check through your story and underline any words that are spelt incorrectly. Write these words in your spelling journal and practise spelling them correctly.

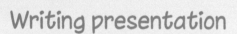

Clauses

The Troll Queen cannot get the stain out of the shirt. Rose steps forward and says, "May I try to wash the shirt?" Rose was taught the simple rhyme below. She says it as she washes the shirt clean.

The old woman must stand at the tub, tub, tub,
The dirty clothes to rub, rub, rub;
But when they are clean and fit to be seen,
She'll dress like a lady and dance on the green.

From North Child *by Edith Pattou*

Talk Partners

Read the rhyme above with your partner. As you speak it alternate clapping together your right hands then left hands, clapping in between. When you have practised this, perform it for the rest of the class.

1 Use a different **coordinating conjunction** to link the two clauses in each of these sentences.

a My brother likes swimming _____ he doesn't go very often.
b The baklava was sweet _____ delicious.
c Mum did not eat her pudding _____ I got a spoon and ate it myself.
d We could not go out to walk _____ it was raining.

2 Underline the **subordinating connective** in these sentences.

a We played golf while dad cooked supper.
b The shop was closed although it was only two o'clock.
c We are going on a ferry even though my brother gets seasick.
d I haven't seen my sunglasses since we got back from our holiday.

Helpful hints

One way of joining two independent clauses together is to use a comma with one of the seven **coordinating conjunctions**. These are: *for, and, nor, but, or, yet, so.* A good way to remember this is that the initial letter of each of these makes the word FANBOYS. A coordinating conjunction shows that the second clause is of equal importance. Sometimes one of the clauses in a sentence is subordinate (less important). For example: *Jo turned the radio off **because** she did not like the loud music.*

This uses the **subordinating connective** 'because' and the first part of the sentence is emphasised. However, here: *Jo turned the radio off **and** she was happy she did not have to listen to the loud music anymore.*

This uses the **coordinating conjunction** 'and'. Both parts of the sentence are equal.

Semi-colons

I can join clauses in sentences.

I can keep a reading log.

The Troll Queen destroys her own castle and Rose and Myk are trapped beneath an avalanche of ice. They escape and make their way back to Rose's home. Here Myk realises that he does not even know his own name so he returns to the castle, where he lived as a white bear, to search for clues. This extract is written by the white bear.

The sheer rock face showed no sign of an entrance, but then it never had. I thought back to the many times I had gone in and out of that mountain. All I had to do then was just picture the door opening and it did. Perhaps if I tried that now …

I entered.

From North Child *by Edith Pattou*

1 Read the extract above then fill in your reading log. Give two reasons why another reader would want to carry on reading this story. Remember to link this to the characters or events of the tale.

Talk Partners

While the man who was the white bear has gone back to the castle to try to find clues about who he really is, Rose is left at home. Using everything you know about Rose from the story, talk about what you think she will do next.

Helpful hints

Sometimes two clauses are joined using **semi-colons** instead of a connecting word. The semi-colon can be used when the two clauses are independent but have closely related ideas. For example: *I have made the cake; I still need to ice it.*

2 Put a **semi-colon** in the correct place in these sentences.

a They liked the house they decided to buy it.
b Some people write with a word processor others use a pen and paper.
c The sun had not yet risen it was still dark.
d I like to read my brother likes to talk!
e The journey was long it seemed to last forever.

Try this

Write a sentence with a coordinating conjunction and a subordinating connective.

A happy ending

And there he was sitting on the red couch, playing his flauto. There was a large book of music open on the couch beside him. He saw me and stopped playing.

"Charles," he said.

I stared at him,

"My name," he said with a smile that lit his face.

From North Child *by Edith Pattou*

Glossary

flauto: a musical instrument similar to a recorder

1 Read the ending to the story above. Put these events from the story in order.

a The bear remembers how to enter the mountain.
b Rose leaves home so that her family will be safe and well.
c Rose is able to get the candlewax stain out of the shirt.
d The knorr is damaged in a storm.
e The white bear appears on a stormy night.

2 Which of these sentences are correctly punctuated?

a Her brother asked, "how did you reach land after the knorr was damaged at sea?"
b Father said, "We came looking for you as soon as we got your letter!"
c Mother whispered, "We were so worried."
d Rose answered, "it was very frightening. I am so glad I found the land."

Helpful hints

When we write dialogue into a story we sometimes put the identity of the person who spoke first. For example: *He said, "I need to know my name."* After introducing who is speaking and how, we use a comma before the inverted commas. The first word of the speech always starts with a capital letter.

3 Finish your reading log for this book. Remember to include the key events. Would you recommend this book? Who do you think would like to read it?

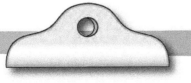

What have I learnt?

Check what you have learnt in this unit.
* I know how to link clauses in a sentence.
* I can keep a reading log which predicts how the story will continue.
* I can use pronouns to replace nouns in a sentence.
* I can use dialogue in a story.

Fiction

Read the story and answer ALL the questions which follow.

Recount – the story of a young evacuee

When mother and father said that my young sister and I had to go and live with our Aunt Amy in Wales for the time being, we were both dismayed and upset. My sister was only nine years old and never liked being away from home, even for just one day, and I knew that our aunt did not really want us, particularly as her own three children were now grown up.

The journey from Liverpool to North Wales, by tram, ferry and bus was a miserable one and parting from mother the next day meant my sister spent the time in tears. I was instructed by my aunt to take her out on to the hill behind the cottage and play some games to try and cheer her up.

The following day we were taken down to the village school, where we met the three teachers and saw our classroom. To us children, used to a large city school, this school was tiny. There were only two large rooms, one for the juniors and seniors and one for the infants. There were no 'proper' desks as we knew them, just a bench for two or three children with a higher bench in front and a shelf for our books underneath. As my sister was rather deaf she had more difficulties than me in trying to adjust.

The 'cottage' was quite large but it had no proper kitchen, no running water and no electricity. We washed in our bedroom in bowls, and water had to be carried up and down. The toilet was half way down the garden and was an earth closet which smelt so much my sister hated it and I had to stand in there with her because she was afraid of the big hole. The lighting was obtained from oil lamps which had to be constantly cleaned and it was quite hard to read as the light given off was so poor.

1 Use a pronoun to complete these sentences. (3)
  a The children went to stay with _____ aunt.
  b "_____ sister is younger than me," I said.
  c The new school was different to the one _____ had attended in Liverpool.
  d The children could put _____books on the shelves.
  e My sister was in the classroom next to _____.

2 Make these words into plurals. (3)
  a One ferry, two _____
  b One shelf, two _____
  c One classroom, two _____
  d One child, two _____
  e One difficulty, two _____

3 Write a synonym for each of these words (3)
  a miserable
  b tiny
  c instructed
  d difficulties
  e afraid

4 Which paragraph in this recount tells how the family lived? (1)

5 Find and write down a phrase which tells the reader the journey was long. (1)

6 Put commas into these sentences so that they are clearer for the reader. (3)
  a The children would like to return home where they can live with their mum.
  b The oil lamps which provided the light had to be cleaned regularly.
  c Our aunt whose children were grown up did not really want us to stay.

7 Underline the prepositions in these sentences. (3)
  a The books were under the desks.
  b There was no running water in the cottage.
  c The oil lamps were near the window.
  d We went to play on the hill.
  e The toilet was in the garden.

8 Write this sentence as direct speech. Remember to use correct punctuation. (1)

  Mum asked me to look after my sister.

9 Put apostrophes in the correct places in these sentences. (3)
  a My aunt is my Mums sister.
  b She really didnt like using the earth closet.
  c The childrens new school was very small.
  d My sisters toys were left behind.
  e Auntys cottage was quite large.

10 Write this recount as a diary entry at the time. Remember that the writer is about (4)
  ten years old and has just had to leave home in Liverpool because of the war.
  Include personal feelings and thoughts.

Fiction

Read the story and answer ALL the questions which follow.

The Lion's Share

One day, a lion, a fox, a jackal, and a wolf all went hunting together. Throughout the long day they hunted, but could not find anything. It was late in the afternoon that they caught a deer. Then they decided to share their food.

The lion was the lord of the jungle and superior to all in strength. The other creatures agreed when he suggested that he be responsible for sharing the food out for everyone.

Placing one of his paws upon the dead deer, the lion announced:

"As one of the hunting party, I will receive one portion."

The others all nodded in agreement.

"But then, I am also the King of Beasts. So I must receive a little bit more," he declared.

The others, now uneasy, looked at each other.

"And besides, I was leading the hunt. So I deserve a little extra," he proclaimed.

The others mumbled something, but it could not be heard.

"As for the fourth share, if you wish to argue with me about its ownership, let's begin, and we will see who will get it."

The other creatures grumbled but they walked away with their heads down. They knew it was pointless to argue.

You may share the labours of the great, but you cannot share the spoils.

1   How do you know that this extract is a fable?   (1)

2   Punctuate these sentences with commas to separate the clauses.   (3)
    a   The lion who was King of the Beasts joined the hunting party.
    b   The four animals now hungry continued with the hunt.
    c   The lion as leader of the hunt took an extra share.
    d   It was late in the afternoon when the beasts had almost given up that they spotted
        a deer.
    e   The lion's share which was almost all of the prey left very little for the other
        animals.

3   Turn this direct speech from the lion into reported speech.
    "And besides, I was leading the hunt. So I deserve a little extra," he proclaimed. (1)

4   What is meant by 'the lion's share?'   (1)
    a   The food the lion eats
    b   The best part
    c   The biggest part
    d   An equal part

5   Find and copy three different words the writer
    has used to show how the lion speaks.   (1)

6   Explain why the writer has used the words you have found for question 5.   (1)

7   Write a pronoun which could be used in the space in these sentences.   (5)
    a   When the animals met, _____ were all hungry.
    b   "As King of the Beasts I will lead," _____ said.
    c   "Follow _____ ," said the lion.
    d   "_____ have hunted all day and are still hungry," grumbled the creatures.
    e   "He has cheated _____," they said as they went home.

8   Punctuate this speech correctly.

    Meet in the forest at first light said the lion and we will hunt for prey.   (1)

9   Explain why the lion placed his great paw on the deer.   (1)

10 Imagine you are the wolf at the end of the day.
    Tell this story to the rest of the pack on your return.   (4)

Unit 7 Dramatic conventions

Charlie and the Chocolate Factory – the play

The story *Charlie and the Chocolate Factory* by Roald Dahl has been made into a play and a film. This is the start of the playscript.

NARRATOR *enters in front of curtain.*

NARRATOR: Welcome to the tale of a delicious adventure in a wonderful land. You can tell it will be delicious – can't you smell it already? (*Sniffs*) Oh, how I love that gorgeous smell! You've all heard of Cadbury's, Rowntree, Fry's, Nestles, Wonka – what's that? You say, what's Wonka? You mean you *don't* know what Wonka is? Why … Wonka Chocolate … of course! I admit that Willy Wonka's Chocolate is fairly new but it's also the greatest chocolate ever invented. Why, Willy Wonka himself is the most amazing, the most fantastic, the most extraordinary chocolate maker the world has ever seen.

… Mr Willy Wonka, in order to sell a lot of candy once again, was running a contest. Yes sir, that's right … a contest! He had secretly wrapped a Golden Ticket under ordinary wrapping paper in five ordinary candy bars… The five winners will tour Mr Wonka's new factory and take home enough chocolate for the rest of their lives. Now *that,* my friends, is where our story begins. Four of the tickets have already been found. Oh, by the way, would you like to meet the four lucky people? All right, listen and watch carefully! I think they're here somewhere. (*Looks out over audience*) Let's see … *Augustus Gloop!* Where are you, Augustus Gloop?

AUGUSTUS GLOOP (*From somewhere in audience*): Chocolate … chocolate … CHOCOLATE!!!

From Charlie and the Chocolate Factory *by Roald Dahl, A play adapted by Richard George.*

Helpful hints

The **playscript** shows who is speaking, what they say and also includes some stage directions. The narrator is 'setting the scene' by explaining to the audience what has happened in the story so far.

Talk Partners

With your partner read through the extract above and write notes on the information the narrator has given the audience which comes from the story. Start like this:

1. This is an adventure story set in a wonderful place.
2. Willy Wonka makes delicious chocolate.
3.

Talk about whether you got all of the information you needed. Think of one question that you would like to ask the narrator.

1 Read the narrator's speech from the beginning to the line where Augustus Gloop is asked to reveal himself. Practise how this would be performed, thinking about the actions the narrator would use. Perform this for the rest of the class.

Charlie and the Chocolate Factory – the book

This is the start of the book *Charlie and the Chocolate Factory.*

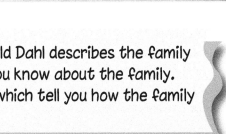

These two very old people are the father and mother of Mr Bucket. Their names are Grandpa Joe and Grandma Josephine.

And *these* two very old people are the father and mother of Mrs Bucket. Their names are Grandpa George and Grandma Georgina.

This is Mr Bucket. This is Mrs Bucket. Mr and Mrs Bucket have a small boy whose name is Charlie Bucket.

This is Charlie.

How d'you do? And how d'you do? And how d'you do again. He is pleased to meet you.

The whole of this family – the six grown-ups (count them) and little Charlie Bucket – live together in a small wooden house on the edge of a great town.

The house wasn't nearly large enough for so many people, and life was extremely uncomfortable for them all. There were only two rooms in the place altogether, and there was only one bed. The bed was given to the four old grandparents because they were so old and tired. They were so tired they never got out of it.

Mr and Mrs Bucket slept in the other room, upon mattresses on the floor.

From the book Charlie and the Chocolate Factory *by Roald Dahl*

Read the extract above. Talk about how Roald Dahl describes the family and their home. Make notes about what you know about the family. Begin like this: six adults, one child. Are there any words which tell you how the family feel about how they live?

1 Change the underlined word in these sentences to a **reflexive pronoun** from the cloud below.

> herself   ourselves   itself   yourself

a The light will turn <u>the light off</u> when no one is in the room.
b You and I have to ask <u>you and I</u> if we have enough time.
c Jia brushed <u>Jia</u> down before she got back on her bicycle after falling off.
d Make sure you clean <u>you</u> up before going to bed.

Helpful hints

Reflexive pronouns refer back to the subject of the sentence. For example: *I walked to school all by <u>myself</u> today.*

97

Willy Wonka's Chocolate Factory – the film

I can compare the print and film versions of a novel.

The film starts off in a candy shop. Children are shown eagerly clamouring and shouting to buy Wonka's candy bars, with names such as 'squelchy snorters' and 'scrumdidilyumptious bars'. There is mayhem as children try to get the sweets they want.

1 The children ask for a 'squelchy snorter'. The letters **sque** are in other spellings. Match these words to their meaning.

squeamish   squeal   squeeze   squelch

a   A high pitched noise   b   A soft sucking sound
c   Easily made to feel sick   d   Press together

2 The very first scene set by the author is very different in the book and film. Copy the table and tick the column to show the words which apply to each version.

	Book	Film
noisy		
crowded		
excitable		
uncomfortable		
poor		

Talk Partners

Talk about what Charlie would say if he went into the candy shop. What words would he use to describe it? Write down one sentence, in properly punctuated direct speech, that Charlie would say about the shop to his family.

3 In the play the narrator involves the audience directly as well as giving information about the story. Write which of these phrases **addresses the audience** or **gives information**.
a   can't you smell it already?
b   it's also the greatest chocolate ever invented.
c   the most extraordinary chocolate maker the world has ever seen.
d   Yes sir, that's right …
e   would you like to meet the four lucky people?

Using mime

Charlie's Birthday

"Happy Birthday!" cried the four old grandparents as Charlie came into their room early the next morning.

Charlie smiled nervously and sat down on the edge of the bed. He was holding his present, his only present, very carefully in his two hands.

WONKA'S WHIPPLESCRUMPTIOUS FUDGEMALLOW DELIGHT, it said on the wrapper.

The four old people, two at either end of the bed, propped themselves up on their pillows and stared with anxious eyes at the bar of chocolate in Charlie's hands.

Mr and Mrs Bucket came in and stood at the foot of the bed, watching Charlie.

The room became silent. Everyone was waiting now for Charlie to start opening his present. Charlie looked down at the bar of chocolate. He ran his fingers slowly back and forth along the length of it, stroking it lovingly, and the shiny paper made little sharp crackly noises in the quiet room.

From the book Charlie and the Chocolate Factory *by Roald Dahl*

Talk Partners

Read the extract above. Think about a special present you have received. Mime for your partner the size and shape of it. Mime unwrapping the present and try to show your partner what the present is. Decide between you on an unusual present. Practise a mime where one of you gives it to the other, show its weight and size by your actions. Mime unwrapping the present for the rest of the class to guess what it is.

1 There are lots of words which are homophones in the extract above. Complete these sentences using a homophone for the underlined word.
  a The <u>four</u> old people bought a present _____ Charlie.
  b <u>Two</u> people gave the gift _____ the boy.
  c The boy <u>rode</u> his bicycle along the _____.
  d <u>Where</u> are the shoes you want to _____.
  e Please <u>write</u> your name on the _____-hand side of the paper.

2 Rewrite these phrases using a possessive apostrophe. See the Helpful hints box on page 57. For example, *The grandparents of Charlie.* → *Charlie's grandparents.*
  a the bed of the grandparents   b the home of the family
  c the job of the father   d the wrapper of the chocolate bar

Writing the story

I can compare book and playscript versions of the same event.

Bucket home, several days later. GRANDPARENTS, MR *and* MRS BUCKET, *as before.*

MR BUCKET: You know, it sure would have been nice if Charlie had won that fifth Golden Ticket.

MRS BUCKET: You mean with that 10p we gave him for his birthday present yesterday?

MR BUCKET: Yes, the one we gave him to buy the one piece of candy he gets every year.

GRANDMA GEORGINA: And just think how long it took you two to save that 10p.

GRANDPA GEORGE: Yes, now that was really a shame.

GRANDMA JOSEPHINE: But think of how Charlie enjoyed the candy. He just loves Willy Wonka chocolate.

MRS BUCKET: He didn't really *act* that disappointed.

MR BUCKET: No, he didn't –

GRANDPA JOE: Well, he might not have acted disappointed, but that's because he's a fine boy and wouldn't want any of us to feel sorry for him. Why – what boy wouldn't be disappointed? I sure wish he'd won. I'd do anything for that boy. Why, I'd even –

CHARLIE (*Running in excitedly*): Mum! Dad! Grandpa Joe! Grandfolks! You'll never believe it!

From Charlie and the Chocolate Factory *by Roald Dahl, A play adapted by Richard George.*

1 Read the playscript extract above and compare it with the book extract on page 99. Copy and complete the table below to show what happens in each version.

Event	Book	Playscript
Charlie is given a chocolate bar for his birthday.		
Charlie uses money he is given to buy a chocolate bar.		
The family talk about what happened the day before.		
The family watch Charlie open his present.		
Charlie has a surprise for everyone.		

2 The playscript includes directions for the actors in brackets. For example: **CHARLIE** (*Running in excitedly*): Add directions for the actors to these lines.

  a   MR BUCKET: You know, it sure would have been nice if Charlie had won that fifth Golden Ticket.

  b   GRANDMA GEORGINA: And just think how long it took you two to save that 10p.

  c   MRS BUCKET: He didn't really *act* that disappointed.

  d   GRANDPA JOE: Well, he might not have acted disappointed, but that's because he's a fine boy and wouldn't want any of us to feel sorry for him.

Writing presentation

Rewrite this section of the playscript from activity 2 as a story. Remember to use direct speech and to punctuate it properly.

Descriptions

Charlie does find the last Golden Ticket and joins the tour of the chocolate factory with four other children and their families. Willy Wonka leads them into the Chocolate Room. This description is from the book.

The Chocolate Room

They were looking down upon a lovely valley. There were green meadows on either side of the valley and along the bottom of it there flowed a great brown river.

What is more, there was a tremendous waterfall halfway along the river – a steep cliff over which the water curled and rolled in a solid sheet, and then went crashing down into a boiling churning whirlpool of froth and spray.

Below the waterfall (and this was the most astonishing sight of all), a whole mass of enormous glass pipes were dangling down into the river from somewhere high up in the ceiling. They really were enormous, those pipes. There must have been a dozen of them at least, and they were sucking up the brownish, muddy water from the river and carrying it away to goodness knows where.

From Charlie and the Chocolate Factory *by Roald Dahl*

1 Use the description above to draw the Chocolate Room. Add something of your own to the picture – something to add some colour and make the room even more astonishing. Write a description of what you have drawn. Read this out to the rest of the class.

Talk Partners

Talk to your partner about an amazing place that you know, perhaps a place you have visited or one you have seen a picture of. Describe it to your partner – think about the colour, the smells, the way it made you feel.

Helpful hints

An **expanded noun phrase** adds information to nouns. You can put the extra information before or after the noun (or both). For example: 'the house' can be expanded to 'the white house' or 'the house on top of the hill' or 'the white house on top of the hill'.

2 Add one of these groups of words to each of the sentences below to make an expanded noun phrase.

> smallest of the litter   new range of   the street corner
> work all day   lived next door

a   The hungry boy was standing on _____.
b   The _____ chocolate bars was delicious.
c   The busy mum was at _____.
d   The young family who _____.
e   The _____ was a beautiful kitten with big green eyes.

Speech

The characters enter the Chocolate Room in the play.

The Chocolate Room. The Chocolate River runs across the stage, surrounded by trees and pipes. All enter as scene opens.

GRANDPA JOE: He said that the rooms we are going to see are enormous. *Some* are supposed to be larger than football fields!

WILLY WONKA: Here we are everybody! This is the Chocolate Room. This room is the nerve centre of the whole factory. It's the heart of my whole operation!

AUGUSTUS GLOOP: Uhh ... I don't see anything but that old river over there. Where's the food? I'm hungry!

MRS GLOOP: And just look at those enormous pipes over there. There must be ten or eleven of them. I wonder what they're for?

CHARLIE: Gee, Mr Wonka, what's wrong with your river? It's all brown and muddy-looking.

WILLY WONKA: *Nothing* wrong with it, my boy! *Nothing!* Nothing at all! It's all chocolate! Every drop of that river is hot melted chocolate of the finest quality. The *very finest* quality.

From Charlie and the Chocolate Factory *by Roald Dahl, A play adapted by Richard George.*

1 Read the extract above. This scene describes the Chocolate Room, with the Chocolate River running through it. What would you use to make each of these props for the play?

a   the Chocolate River   b   trees

Write down your ideas for the props, including a labelled diagram.

Talk Partners

Imagine you were in the group going around the factory. Talk to your partner about your reaction when you enter the Chocolate Room and what you would say.

2 Rewrite this scene with you in it. Include what you say and give some idea of how you feel about the Chocolate Room.

3 Write a short conversation between Willy Wonka and Charlie as they enter the Chocolate Room. Remember to punctuate your work using speech marks and to use adverbs to describe how they both spoke. Begin like this:

"And, this is the amazing Chocolate Room," announced Willy Wonka proudly.

Using words for effect

In the book Willy Wonka talks about the chocolate waterfall.

"The waterfall is most important!" Mr Wonka went on. "It mixes the chocolate! It churns it up! It pounds and beats it! It makes it light and frothy! No other factory in the world mixes its chocolate by waterfall! But it's the only way to do it properly! The only way!"

From Charlie and the Chocolate Factory *by Roald Dahl*

Talk Partners

Read the extract above and speak the words in the extract out loud to your partner. Miss out `Mr Wonka went on`. Discuss how the punctuation makes you speak the words. What tone do you use?

1 Write two diary entries for Charlie. The first one is the evening before his visit to the Chocolate Factory. Write the second entry about what he sees in the Chocolate Room. Remember to include how he is feeling in both entries.

2 Willy Wonka explains that the waterfall 'churns' the chocolate. Synonyms for churn are 'whisk' and 'beat'. Give two synonyms for each of these verbs.

  a dash
  b fling
  c slither
  d swirl
  e creep

Helpful hints

A **narrator** is a person who gives a **commentary** (an account) on what is happening in a film or play. This helps the viewer to understand what is happening.

Talk Partners

Read the text on page 102. Discuss how you would write a commentary on the visitors entering the Chocolate Room. Remember to think about all of the characters, describe how they entered the room and what their reactions are.

Writing presentation

Write up the commentary you have discussed with your talk partner, with you as the narrator. Begin like this: Willy Wonka entered the room followed by …

New words

This is how the Oompa-Loompas are introduced in the play.

VERUCA SALT (*Screaming as she looks over the edge of the river*): Look! Look over there! What is it? He's moving! He's walking! Why, it's a little person! It's a little man! Down there behind one of the pipes!

(*Everyone rushes to the edge of the river to get a better look*)

CHARLIE: She's right, Grandpa! It *is* a little man! Can you see him?

GRANDPA JOE: I see him, Charlie! ...

CHARLIE: Aren't they fantastic?

GRANDPA JOE: No higher than my knee!

CHARLIE: Look at their funny long hair! They can't be *real* people!

WILLY WONKA: Nonsense! Of course they are real people! They are some of my workers!

MIKE TEAVEE: That's impossible! There are no people in the world as small as that!

WILLY WONKA: No people in the world as small as that? Then let me tell you something. There are more than three thousand of them in my factory! They are Oompa-Loompas!

CHARLIE: Oompa-Loompas! What do you mean?

WILLY WONKA: Imported direct from Loompaland. And oh, what a terrible country it is! Nothing but thick jungles infested by the most dangerous beasts in the world – hornswogglers and snozzwangers and those terrible wicked whangdoodles. A whangdoodle would eat ten Oompa-Loompas for breakfast then come galloping back for a second helping.

From Charlie and the Chocolate Factory *by Roald Dahl, A play adapted by Richard George.*

1 Write notes about the Oompa-Loompas from this script above. Divide your notes into two headings: **Appearance**   **Where from**

Talk Partners Share your notes with your talk partner. Did you both write the same things? You have written facts from the playscript. Now use the information to give your opinion about what the visitors think about the Oompa-Loompas. Can you tell what everyone thinks?

Talk Partners Discuss with your talk partner what you think the whangdoodles, hornswogglers and snozzwangers look like, what they eat and how they act. Choose one and write your description. Use adjectives.

Storyboard

This extract is taken from the book.

The Chocolate River

"Be careful Augustus," shouted Mrs Gloop. "You're leaning too far out!"
Mrs Gloop was absolutely right. For suddenly there was a shriek, and
then a splash, and into the river went Augustus Gloop, and in one
second he had disappeared under the brown surface.
"Save him!" screamed Mrs Gloop, going white in the face, and waving
her umbrella about.
"He'll drown. He can't swim a yard! Save him! Save him!"
"Good heavens, woman," said Mr Gloop. "I'm not diving in there! I've got my best suit on!"

...

Then all at once the powerful suction took hold of him completely, and he was pulled under the
surface and then into the mouth of the pipe.
The crowd on the riverbank waited breathlessly to see where he would come out.
'There he goes!" somebody shouted, pointing upwards.
And sure enough, because the pipe was made of glass, Augustus Gloop could be seen shooting up
inside it, head first, like a torpedo.
"Help! Murder! Police!" screamed Mrs Gloop. "Augustus, come back at once! Where are you going?"

From Charlie and the Chocolate Factory *by Roald Dahl*

Helpful hints

1 Read the extract above.
Use a storyboard to
show how you would
plan the filmscript
version of this part of the
story. Think about the
key events and the
important characters as
the scene unfolds. Write

Actions: (Augustus reaches out to touch the chocolate river). Script: MRS GLOOP: Augustus, Augustus darling. I don't think you should do that. Tell him Mr Wonka!	Actions: Script: _____ _____ _____ _____

A **film script** has the words
which the characters will
speak but the director will tell
the actors how to act. Only
the actors who are in camera
shot can be seen.

the character's lines and actions. The first box has been started for you.

2 In this extract there is an example of a simile –
like a torpedo. Write similes for these phrases:
a He fell into the water with a splash like
_____.
b As white in the face as _____.
c Waving her umbrella like _____.
d The crowd on the riverbank waited as
quietly as _____.

3 Copy each sentence and underline
the metaphors.
a As they gazed across the water,
the peaceful lake was a mirror.
b Compared to the rest of the school,
our class is a peaceful oasis.
c Tom is a pussy cat at home, you
wouldn't think he is so competitive.

The character's viewpoint

The Chocolate River

(AUGUSTUS GLOOP *leans over river*)

MRS GLOOP: Augustus! Augustus, sweetheart! I don't think you had better do that.

WILLY WONKA: Oh, no! Please, Augustus, p-l-e-a-s-e! I beg of you not to do that. My chocolate must be untouched by human hands!

MRS GLOOP: Augustus! Didn't you hear what the man said? Come away from that river at once!

AUGUSTUS GLOOP (*Leaning over further*): This stuff is *teee-rrific!* Oh boy, I need a bucket to drink it properly!

WILLY WONKA: Augustus … you *must* come away! *You are dirtying my chocolate!*

MRS GLOOP: Augustus! You'll be giving that nasty cold of yours to about a million people all over the country! Be careful Augustus! You're leaning *too far out!!*

(AUGUSTUS *shrieks as he falls in*)

MRS GLOOP: Save him! He'll drown! He can't swim a yard! Save him! Save him!

AUGUSTUS GLOOP: Help! Help! Fish me out!

MRS GLOOP: (*To everybody*): Don't just stand there! *Do* something!

VERUCA SALT: Look! He's being sucked closer to one of the pipes!

From Charlie and the Chocolate Factory *by Roald Dahl, A play adapted by Richard George.*

Talk Partners

Read the extract above. Talk about how this part of the play might look if it were a film. Discuss what you think would be showing on screen at each point in the playscript above.

1

> **MRS. GLOOP:** Augustus! Didn't you hear what the man said? Come away from that river at once!
>
> **AUGUSTUS GLOOP** (*Leaning over further*): This stuff is *teee-rrific!* Oh boy, I need a bucket to drink it properly!

Using these words spoken by Mrs Gloop and Augustus, write a paragraph telling the reader what Augustus is doing, in his own words (from his viewpoint). Remember to include other characters and what they say. Begin like this: *All that lovely chocolate just flowing past me, I am sure Mr Wonka won't notice if …*

Performance

The five Oompa-Loompas start singing and dancing as Mr and Mrs Gloop are led away to find Augustus. This is an extract from their song in the play.

We add some sugar, cream and spice;
Then out he comes! And now! By grace!
A miracle has taken place!
This boy, who only just before
Was loathed by men from shore to shore,
This greedy brute, this louse's ear,
Is loved by people everywhere!
For who could hate or bear a grudge
Against a luscious bit of fudge?

From Charlie and the Chocolate Factory *by Roald Dahl, A play adapted by Richard George.*

Talk Partners

Read the song through together. Work out which words to emphasise and what tone of voice to use where. Divide the song up, speak some lines on your own and some lines together. Add actions and expressions to your performance.

Talk Partners

Talk about how Roald Dahl shows the reader what sort of character Augustus is. Find evidence from the extracts so far to support your view. Draw a picture of Augustus and write your ideas and your evidence around him. For example: If you think Augustus was greedy find evidence in the playscript, the extract from the book and in the song.

1 The Oompa-Loompas plan to change Augustus from a 'greedy brute' who is 'loathed' to someone who is 'loved by people everywhere'. *Loathed* and *loved* are antonyms. Give some interesting antonyms for these words:

a muffled   b grimy   c ghastly   d bulky   e sparkling

2 Earlier you wrote a diary entry telling what Charlie could see in the Chocolate Room (activity 1 on page 103). Now add to that entry telling the event of Augustus being sucked up the tube. Remember to write from Charlie's point of view and to include his feelings and thoughts.

Violet's character

This extract from the play helps to show Violet's character.

WILLY WONKA: … This piece of gum I've just made happens to be tomato soup, roast beef, *and* blueberry pie! But you can have almost anything you want!

VIOLET BEAUREGARDE: What do you mean by that?

WILLY WONKA: If you were to start chewing it, you would actually taste *all* of those things. *And* it fills you up! It satisfies you! It's terrific!

VERUCA SALT: It's utterly impossible!

VIOLET BEAUREGARDE: Just so long as it's gum, and I can chew it … then that's for me! (*She takes her own piece of gum out of her mouth and sticks it behind her left ear*) Come on, Mr Wonka, hand over this magic gum of yours … and we'll see if the thing works!

MRS BEAUREGARDE: Now, Violet … let's not do anything silly.

VIOLET BEAUREGARDE: I want the gum! What's so silly?

WILLY WONKA: I would rather you didn't take it. You see, I haven't got it quite right yet. There are still one or two things –

VIOLET BEAUREGARDE: (*Interrupting*): Oh, to heck with that!

(*She grabs the gum and pops it into her mouth*)

WILLY WONKA: Don't!

From Charlie and the Chocolate Factory *by Roald Dahl, A play adapted by Richard George.*

1 Read the extract above. Change these examples of direct speech to reported speech.
  a "You can have almost anything you want!" explained Mr Wonka.
  b "I want the gum!" Violet said obstinately.
  c "I would rather you didn't take it," Mr Wonka told her gently.
  d "The gum isn't ready yet!" warned Mr Wonka.

Talk Partners Using what you already know from when Augustus did not follow Willy Wonka's advice, talk with your partner about what you think will happen now to Violet. If you know what happens next, make up something new.

2 From the extract above, write what you know about Violet. You can deduce things from the way that she acts – give evidence to support your statements. For example, *Violet is rude, she demands the gum from Willy Wonka without saying please.*

Word meanings

I can write comparatives.

I can add a suffix to change the meaning of a word.

1 Continue writing Charlie's diary (from activity 2 on page 107). Add the incident with Violet and the chewing gum. Remember to include his own thoughts and viewpoint on what has happened.

Helpful hints

The main points in a story are called **key events**. These must be kept in when a story is made into a play or a film.

Talk Partners Talk with your partner about the key events in the story.

2 Write the comparative for each of these words. The first one has been done for you.
a chewy – *chewier*
b tasty
c proud
d angry
e plump

Helpful hints

Adding **–er** to the words in activity 2 makes the words comparatives. The new gum was chewier – which means it was more chewy.
Don't forget that if the word ends in **y**, you change the **y** to an **i** before adding **–er**. Some words cannot have **–er** added to them so the word 'more' is used. For example, *anxious* needs to be written as *more anxious*.

3 Work out which of these words can be made into a comparative by adding **–er** and which must have 'more' written with them. Copy and complete the table.

word	er	more
happy		
inquisitive		
excited		
nervous		
loud		

4 In the film Violet says "I don't care" when Willy Wonka tells her the gum is not ready yet. By eating the gum she is careless (without care).
Add the suffix 'less' to these words and then write them into a sentence.
a fear
b worth
c end
d taste
e power

Charlie's character

As the tour continues the children all do something which has disastrous results and they are taken away by the Oompa-Loompas to be cured. Eventually only Charlie is left. This is from the final scene in the play.

WILLY WONKA: Well … of course Charlie and all of the others will receive all of the candy I promised, but I want *Charlie* to receive *much more*! You see, this whole day has been a *contest*. It's been a contest to find out who would be the best person for the job.

CHARLIE: What job?

WILLY WONKA: Well you see, I'm tired, Charlie. I'm not getting any younger, and it isn't as easy to carry out my ideas as … as… it once was. I need some help. That means… *you!*

CHARLIE: Me?

WILLY WONKA: Yes! I would like you and Grandpa Joe and, of course, all the rest of your family, to move here – and live here – *permanently!*

From Charlie and the Chocolate Factory *by Roald Dahl, A play adapted by Richard George.*

Talk Partners

Read the extract above. Talk about Charlie. What sort of character is he? Use all of the extracts to support your views. Compare him to the other characters, for example, he did not snatch the gum like Violet.

Talk Partners

Charlie is surprised to hear that he has won the contest. With your partner show surprise by the way that you look. Use your whole body to show these feelings:

a excited
b embarrassed
c puzzled
d angry
e disappointed

Try this

Can you think of a different feeling you can mime? Practise it first then show the class. Can they guess what you are miming?

 1 Finish Charlie's diary, including him winning the contest. Remember to include Charlie's viewpoint.

Willy Wonka's character

1 Willy Wonka is a central character in the story. Draw a picture of him and write what you know about him around it. Support your ideas with evidence from all of the extracts.

2 Use adverbs to show how the characters speak in these sentences:
a "Augustus do be careful," Mum called _____.
b "Help him, he can't swim," she pleaded _____.
c "I have the record for chewing gum the longest," Violet said _____.
d "My invention will mean no more cooking!" Wonka boasted _____.

3 Write a preposition into the gap in these sentences:
a The Oompa-Loompas were standing on the _____ of the Chocolate River.
b Willy Wonka led the visitors _____ the factory.
c The group met at the factory gates _____ nine o'clock.
d Augustus travelled _____ the glass pipes.

Talk Partners Imagine that after the tour a newspaper reporter wants to interview Charlie. Take a part each, one as the reporter and one as Charlie. Think of the questions to ask and answers you would give. Make notes for yourselves and practise the interview. Remember to stay in character. Perform the interview for the rest of the class.

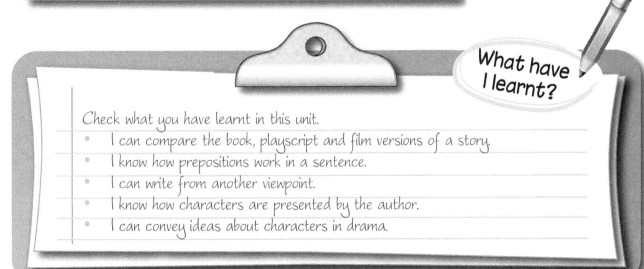

What have I learnt?

Check what you have learnt in this unit.
* I can compare the book, playscript and film versions of a story.
* I know how prepositions work in a sentence.
* I can write from another viewpoint.
* I know how characters are presented by the author.
* I can convey ideas about characters in drama.

 Instructions

Planting courgette seeds

I know how instructions are written.

I can listen carefully.

Courgettes are also known as zucchini. They are the most popular vegetable of the squash family. They have a deep green skin with a pale flesh and are easy to cook.

Courgette plants grow very big and need a large space to sprawl over. However, it is possible to start the plants growing in small containers on a sunny window ledge.

You will need:
- Compost
- Courgette seeds
- Small pots (plastic drinking cups or old yoghurt pots can be used)
- Water

What to do
1. Fill the pots to about 6 cm below the top with compost.
2. Place a seed in the compost.
3. Top up with another 3–4 cm of compost.
4. Water carefully.
5. Place on a tray on a sunny window ledge.
6. Check every day. Keep the soil moist but not soggy. (Touch the compost gently – if a little sticks to your finger do not give any more water.)
7. After about two months from planting the seeds, transplant the plants into the garden. Dig a hole slightly bigger than the pots, gently place the plant in the hole and put soil tightly around it. Water well.

Remember to wash your hands after handling the compost. Enjoy the courgettes you grow. Harvest them when they are about 12 cm long and add them to all sorts of exciting recipes.

Talk Partners

Read the instructions above. They contain some handy hints for the gardener. Read them through with your partner and discuss which are instructions and which are handy hints.

Imperative verbs

1 Find the imperative verbs in the instructions on how to plant courgette seeds on page 112. Write these in your books.

2 Choose the correct word for each definition.

> squabble   squadron   squall
>   square   equal

a A shape with four sides of equal length.
b An argument.
c A sudden rise in wind speed.
d The same as.
e Part of a navy fleet.

3 These instructions on how to cook a recipe which includes courgettes have become muddled up. Number them so that they are in the correct order.

a Put the garlic and cheese in a bowl and mix them together. This makes a garlic cheese mix.
b First heat the oven to 350°F, 180°C, gas mark 4.
c Secondly slice the tomatoes.
d Finally finish with a layer of the garlic cheese mix and bake in the hot oven for about 30 minutes.
e Put the sliced courgettes in a bowl and mix them with three spoonsful of olive oil. Leave them while you make the garlic cheese mix.
f Oil an ovenproof dish and start layering the vegetables, starting with a layer of fried courgettes, then a layer of tomatoes and a sprinkle of the garlic cheese mix.
g Thirdly slice the courgettes thinly lengthways.
h Fry the marinated courgettes until soft.

Helpful hints

Instructions tell you what to do. The words which do this are **imperative verbs**, which give an instruction, such as 'Place…'.

Courgettes are from the **squ**ash family of vegetables. The letters **qua** are in the words in activity 2. Recognising these letters will help you to spell other words which have this letter combination.

Glossary

marinade: a liquid in which meat, fish or vegetables are soaked before cooking in order to flavour or soften them

Suffixes

1 The courgettes are sliced thin**ly**. The suffix –**ly** has been added to the word 'thin' to tell us how they were cut. Rewrite the sentences below using an –**ly** word which means the same as the words underlined.

  a   He plays football <u>every week</u>.
  b   The children went camping <u>every year</u>.
  c   The bread was sliced very <u>thick</u>.
  d   We have a new book <u>every month</u>.
  e   The class cheered <u>out loud</u> when they won the competition.

Helpful hints

Adding the suffix -**ly** to a word usually tells us how or how often something is done.

2 Add the suffix –**ly** to these words. Use the rule shown opposite in the Helpful hints box.

  a   angry   b   busy
  c   happy   d   grumpy
  e   hungry

Helpful hints

When the suffix -**ly** is added to a word which already ends in the letter **y** the original **y** is taken away and replaced with an **i**. For example: noisy – remove the y, add ily → noisily.

Talk Partners

Write down as many words as you can think of together which end in `ful' and could have –**ly** added. For example: graceful – gracefully. Share your words with the rest of the class and listen carefully to everyone else's list.

3 Underline the words in the sentences below which have 'silent' vowels (vowels we don't say) in them.

  a   The temperature was very high in the classroom.
  b   You can get books about cooking from the library reference section.
  c   A tortoise is an interesting animal.
  d   The children were miserable because they could not go out to play.
  e   Everyone enjoyed the marvellous food.

Writing a recipe

I can use more specialised vocabulary to match the topic.

Talk Partners

With your talk partner make a list of the ingredients and equipment you would need to make the recipe on page 113. Use the specific words (vocabulary) for this. For example, the recipe refers to a griddle pan and marinade. Give the dish a name.

1 Work together to write out the whole recipe, including ingredients and equipment needed.

2 Use this checklist to help you write your recipe instructions.

Features of instructional text	
Have you included a title which tells you what is to be achieved?	✓
Do the instructions tell you what to do – one step at a time?	✓
Have you included a labelled diagram?	✓
Is the language used simple to understand?	✓
Have you used imperative verbs (verbs which tell you what to do)?	✓
Is it written in the second person?	✓
Have you only included the necessary details?	✓
Have you used numbers (1,2, …) or time connectives (then, next…)?	✓

3 Write down what the pronoun is referring to in each of these instructions.

a I have planted some new trees in the garden to make <u>it</u> more shady.

b Peel the potatoes and place <u>them</u> in a large saucepan.

c Fill the vase with water before arranging the flowers in <u>it</u>.

d Answer the telephone when <u>it</u> rings.

e Check your hands and wash <u>them</u> before eating.

Helpful hints

Instructions are written in the **second person**. This means you are addressing another person and may use the pronouns 'you' or 'your'. For example: *Pour **your** batter in a greased tin and bake in a hot oven.*

Finding lost keys

I can write instructions.

Mum drove Marcos to the park. She parked the car in the car park and they walked to the entrance. They had a lovely day.

At 4 o'clock Mum said, "Time to go. We have to stop at Grandma's on the way home."

When they got back to the car, Mum put her hand in her pocket for the keys. They weren't there! "That's strange. I'm sure I put them in my pocket. Let's see if they are in my bag."

The keys were nowhere to be seen.

"They must have fallen out of my pocket. We will have to go and look for them," said Mum.

Marcos took the map of the park out of his pocket. "Let's retrace our steps," he said.

To make sure that they looked everywhere in the park Marcos gave these instructions:

"Mum, when you go through the entrance keep right. Walk past the blue hut on your right and follow the path so the red and yellow striped tent is on your left. Take the path to the right and walk past the roundabout with the blue and yellow top. Take the next path on the right and keep walking until you reach the fountain. I will meet you there."

Talk Partners

Follow the instructions Marcos gave his mother by tracing where she will walk with your finger. Discuss which part of the park has not been searched and describe what she has passed on her route.

 Marcos must search the area that is left. Starting at the park entrance write the instructions for Marcos which tell him where to walk.

Prefix re-

I can use pronouns in a sentence.

I know more about prefixes.

Talk Partners

Read your instructions from activity 1 on page 116 to your talk partner. Listen carefully and check the map to see if any area has been left out.

1 Choose the correct word for each definition:

revert   refurbish   recede   reflect   rebuild

a   make again
b   go or move back
c   cast a light back from a surface
d   go back to how things were
e   improve on current condition

Helpful hints

Marcos suggested that they **retrace** their steps. This means to go back over the same route. The prefix **re-** can be used in front of words to mean *back* or *again*.

Talk Partners

Discuss this sentence with your talk partner. *When Jasmine and Elisha get home from the concert she will call her mother.* Is it clear who the pronouns 'she' and 'her' are referring to? Rewrite this sentence to make it clear.

2 Possessive pronouns are used to show who owns something. Copy and complete this table showing who is the owner and what is the object.

Sentence	Owner	Object
The dog chased his ball.	*dog*	*ball*
The girls read their books.		
Marcos's mum drove her car.		
The gardener washed his hands.		
The photographer dropped her camera.		

Talking about a party

Talk Partners

With your partner, talk about an occasion when people celebrate with a party. This might be a birthday, a wedding or a festival. Imagine you are planning to have a party. Talk about what you would be celebrating, where you would have the party, when it would be and who you would invite.

1 Write the invitation to the party you have discussed with your talk partner. Remember to include all of the important information. Share your invitation with the rest of the class. Do they have any questions which should have been answered by including more information on the invitation?

Talk Partners

Explain to your talk partner how to get to where the party is being held. Think about where they are setting out from, where they are going and any transport they may need. As you do this your partner must take notes. Swap places and repeat the exercise. Remember to include any landmarks which will help them. For example: the house with the high, red fence.

2 Use the notes you have made with your talk partner to write detailed instructions. Remember to use imperative verbs (**turn** left, **cross** the road) and time connectives (after, then).

3 Instructions have lots of prepositions in them. Underline the prepositions in the instructions below.
a   Put the dish in the oven.
b   Make sure the card is under the material.
c   Stick the plastic discs next to each other.
d   Sprinkle chocolate on top of the pastry.
e   Put it on the ledge after you have painted it.

Helpful hints

A **preposition** is used to show the position of something: *on, under;* the time when something happens: *at, after* and the way in which something is done: *by.* Sometimes more than one word is used: *on top* and this is then called a **prepositional phrase**.

Origami two-fold angelfish

How to make a two-fold angelfish

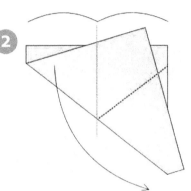

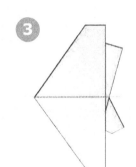

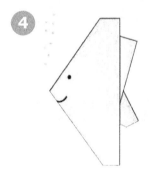

1 Use the instructions above to make the origami angelfish. Use pieces of cotton to hang the fish from the ceiling and make a class aquarium display.

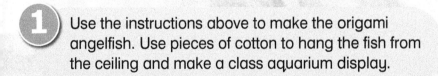

Did you know?

Origami is the traditional Japanese art of paper folding. The aim of this art is to turn a flat sheet of paper into a finished sculpture through folding.

Origami candy cane

1 Begin with a square piece of paper that is coloured on one side and white on the other side. Place the white side facing up.

2 Fold the paper in half to form a triangle but leave a little white border about 1 cm all around.

3 Turn the paper over so that you only see the coloured side.

4 Fold the base of the triangle up a little (about 1cm). You will notice that the tips of the triangle begin to have a coloured-white-coloured pattern.

5 Fold the base of the triangle up again and again.

6 Repeat until the entire triangle has been folded into a striped stick.

7 Depending on the type of paper you use, you may need a small piece of tape to secure the paper so it doesn't unravel.

8 To make the stick into a candy cane, fold a 90 degree angle about a third of the way down. It will look like the letter 'L'.

9 Fold the tip of the letter 'L' up to form a hook. If necessary, use a small piece of tape to keep the shape.

1 Make the paper candy cane using the instructions above. Think about the colour of the paper and how to make it look most effective.

2 Write a simple set of instructions on how to wrap a present. Remember to include what equipment you will need and use imperative verbs at every step.

Talk Partners Discuss with your talk partner whether the candy cane above was hard to make without illustrations. Which set of instructions was the clearest, those for the candy cane or the angelfish on page 119?

Talk Partners Share your instructions with your talk partner. Ask them if you could make any improvements. Redraft your instructions to make them clearer.

3 The word present has many meanings. One meaning is a gift, another that someone/something is in place. Write a sentence for each of these meanings.

Tense agreement

I can make tenses agree in a sentence.

1 The imperative verb is not always at the start of each step in the instructions to make a candy cane on page 120. Reword these instructions to put an imperative verb at the start of each step.

2 These instructions for changing a bicycle tyre do not make sense. Correct them by changing the underlined words.

a If the tyre is <u>blow</u> out, or <u>have</u> a large hole, it will have to be <u>replace</u>.

b Turn the bike over so it is <u>stand</u> on the seat and handlebars.

c Spin the wheel <u>slow</u>, <u>looked</u> for anything <u>stick</u> out like a screw or nail.

d Let the remaining air out of the inner tube. A matchstick can be <u>use</u> for this.

e <u>Taking</u> the tyre off the rim.

3 Copy and complete this table to say if the letter **y** is acting as a vowel or a consonant.

Word	Vowel	Consonant
yellow	*no*	*yes*
symbol		
gym		
yoghurt		
my		
twenty		

Helpful hints

It is important that **instructions** make sense otherwise the person using them will become confused.

Helpful hints

The words *tyre* and *cycle* have the letter **y** in place of the vowel i. In some words **y** is a consonant. The way to tell these apart is to say the word. If **y** sounds like a vowel then in that word it is a vowel. If it sounds like a consonant then in that word it is a consonant.

Talk Partners

With your talk partner make a list of words where the letter **y** is used as a consonant. Share your list with the rest of the class. How many did you find altogether?

Rules for a game

I can write instructions.

Snakes and Ladders game

1. **Assemble the materials.** (A snakes and ladders board, a dice and a coloured counter for each player.)

2. **Understand the goal of the game.** The aim of the game is to be the first player to reach the end by moving around the board from square 1 to square 100. You will travel the board from base to top, right, then left and so on.

3. **Start playing.** The first player to roll the number 6 on the dice can enter the board. Each subsequent player must also throw a 6 to enter the board. The dice must be rolled again to show the number of squares that the player may move. Place the counter on the appropriate square.

4. **Continue playing.** Each player rolls the dice in turn and moves their counter the number of squares that is shown on the dice.
   - *Snake*: if a player lands at the tip of the snake's head, his or her counter slides down to the square at the end of the snake's tail.
   - *Ladder*: if a player lands on a square that is at the base of a ladder, his or her counter moves to the square at the top of the ladder and continues from there.

5. **Complete the game.** The first player to reach square 100 is the winner but must have the correct number on the dice to land on the number 100.

 Read the instructions above. Write the rules to play Snakes and Ladders backwards. For example: The first player to throw a number 1 on the dice, starts on square 100. What other actions need to be reversed?

Talk Partners

With your talk partner make a list of everything you have at home that has a set of instructions with it. Remember to include games, things in the kitchen and media items.
Share your list with the rest of the class and keep a tally count of all the different things people mention.

Possessive apostrophes

I can use possessive apostrophes.

 1 Write a set of instructions for washing your face. Think about the items you will need and the imperative verbs you will use.

Talk Partners
Take it in turns to read your instructions while your talk partner mimes the actions. Perform this for the rest of the class.

 2 Rewrite these sentences using a possessive apostrophe. The first one has been done for you.

a The keyboard on the computer was broken.
The computer's keyboard was broken.
b The door to the shed was open.
c The toys belonging to Nisha are in the garden.
d The petals on the rose smelt lovely.
e The tyre on the blue car has a puncture.

3 Write down whether the apostrophes in these sentences have been used for possession or to show missing letters (contraction).

a The children's coats have their names on them.
b They won't be home until five o'clock.
c The gardener's hands were very muddy.
d There's a new computer in their classroom.

Helpful hints

In the instructions on page 122, the snake's head could have been referred to as the head of a snake. The base of the ladder could have been referred to as the ladder's base. The **possessive apostrophe** is used to show that something belongs to something or somebody.

Homophones are words which sound the same but are spelt differently and have different meanings. For example: *I have a patch on my eye.*

Talk Partners
With your talk partner find homophones for these definitions.

a Detect things with your eyes. /
A place where whales and dolphins live.
b A cooking ingredient made from wheat. /
The colourful part of a plant.
c Light coloured. / A bucket.
d Two that match. / A type of fruit.

Asking questions

How to set up an aquarium

If you're looking to keep a goldfish in an aquarium here is how to make your fish happy and healthy!

1. Buy a tank which is large enough for the number of fish you plan to keep. Be sure to fit a lid.
2. Place the tank out of direct sunlight on a surface strong enough to take its weight.
3. Buy some gravel to put in the bottom of the tank. Make sure that you buy large rocks (too big for a fish swallow) or very small gravel. Goldfish like to dig into the gravel to search for food that has sunk to the bottom.
4. Place a filter in the tank.
5. Fill the tank with water. Put in plants and ornaments for the fish to hide in.
6. Leave for one week before you put the fish in.
7. Feed the fish daily.

Did you know?

The word *aquarium* can also be used to describe a building where transparent tanks of live fish are kept. The word aquarium has the root word **aqua** which means water.

Talk Partners

Read the instructions above. Discuss whether the instructions to set up an aquarium are written well enough for you to know how to ensure that your fish are well and happy. Work together to write down any questions you still have about looking after fish. For example: *Does the tank need cleaning?* Share your questions with the rest of the class and listen carefully to everyone's ideas. Do you know where to find the answers to your questions?

1 Write out the sentences with the correct missing word.

> aquatic   aquarium   aqualung

a A place where marine plants and fish are kept is an _____ .
b A diver wears an _____ when underwater.
c Something which happens in or around water is _____ .

2 Write these sentences with the missing prepositions.
a Provide weeds for the fish to hide _____.
b Just feed fish _____ a day, preferably at the same time every day.
c Check that no food is left floating _____ the water.
d Always keep fish _____ a tank, never a bowl!
e Do not place the tank _____ a window as direct sunlight is harmful.

Reading for clarity

I can check for clarity and purpose.

Daily News
Morning TV Disaster

The TV presenter Eirlys Macdew was covered in fruit smoothie in front of millions of viewers yesterday. Celebrity chef Jez Whittle explained how to make a fruit smoothie using strawberries, banana and ice cream. Unfortunately Eirlys did not listen to all of the instructions.

She put the ingredients into the blender and stopped to make an announcement to the audience. On her return she switched the blender onto full power and she was

splattered in fruit and ice cream! She had forgotten to put the lid on!

The TV audience gasped as Eirlys wiped the mixture from her expensive suit. "It was a shock, the ice cream was so cold and I just wasn't expecting it," she explained.

"It just goes to show that you must listen to instructions carefully," said Jez.

Talk Partners

Read the report above. Discuss with your partner how you can make sure that the instructions you give are clear and that the important actions are carried out.

Fruit smoothie

Ingredients: one small punnet of strawberries, one banana, one carton of ice cream

Equipment: blender, sharp knife, spoon

Instructions

1. Remove the stalks from the strawberries. Cut them into halves and place in the blender.

2. Remove the skin from the banana. Cut it into quarters and place these in the blender.

3. Spoon the ice cream into the blender.

4. Place the lid on the blender. Turn on and leave for 30 seconds.

5. Remove the lid. Pour the smoothie into a glass and enjoy.

 1 Read the instructions for making a smoothie. What effect would missing out the following vital steps have?

a Not removing the stalks from the strawberries.

b Not removing the skin from the banana.

c Not cutting the banana into quarters.

d Forgetting to put the lid on the blender.

e Forgetting to turn the blender on.

Speech

I can use known rules to make words plural and singular.

I can set dialogue out properly.

1 Copy and complete this table to show singular and plural.

Singular	Plural
fly	
	lorries
family	
hobby	
	babies

2 Turn these examples of reported speech into direct speech.

a Petra, a member of the audience, told our reporter that Eirlys screamed at first but then burst out laughing.

b The make-up girl explained that she would have to fix Eirlys's hair during the commercial break.

c Eirlys announced that she would never eat a fruit smoothie again!

d Jez said that he was so pleased the recipe was not hot.

e Our reporter said that the lesson is 'always listen carefully to instructions'.

Helpful hints

The word strawberry ends in the letter y. To make this plural you must take off the letter y and add **ies**.

In the newspaper article on page 125 the presenter and the chef both gave quotes. The actual words they used were written down within speech marks. This is **direct speech**. If the newspaper had used **reported speech** it would have said: *Jez explained that it is important to listen to instructions carefully.*

Which vital step has been missed out from these instructions?

Tying your shoelaces
1. Wrap one lace round the other to tie a half knot.
2. Pull tight.
3. Form a loop with one end.
4. Wrap the other lace around the first loop.
5. Tighten and make the loops and ends all roughly the same length

Can you add the step?

Try this

Greek mosaics

I can use a subordinate clause.

1 First, using colour, draw your own mosaic. Remember each piece will be made up of a small piece of broken tile or pottery. Using your design write an explanation to help another person follow your pattern. For example: *This mosaic is a pattern which is made up of five different coloured pieces. The pattern begins in the top, left-hand corner …*

2 Write these sentences and underline the subordinate clause. Look back at the Helpful hints box on page 89.

  a This mosaic is a pattern which is made up of different coloured pieces.

  b It is made up of small pieces of glass that are all different shades of green and blue.

  c The first line, which is blue, is the start of the sky.

3 Copy and complete these sentences with a subordinating connective from the list below.

| although | if | because |

  a We had to stay indoors today _____ it was too hot outside.

  b I had my lunch early _____ I wasn't really hungry.

  c There will be a rainbow _____ the sun shines while it is raining.

Mosaic is a decorative art which uses small coloured pieces of glass, stone or pottery. The oldest Greek mosaics were made of pebbles and were used for floors and footpaths. Some of the designs can be quite simple patterns, while others are very complicated pictures.

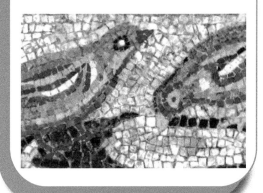

Matching words to their use

Shaun and Roisin were very poor. They lived in a small house. Shaun worked hard every day to grow vegetables for them to eat and Roisin cared for their few animals; a goat who gave them milk; a few hens who laid eggs and a donkey who helped pull the cart to market.

Roisin was worried that the hens would wander off or that a fox would come and harm them in the night.

"Don't worry," said Shaun. "I will build a chicken coop to keep them safe."

Glossary

chicken coop: a shelter that keeps chickens safe from predators. It has an indoor area where the chickens roost (rest) at night and an outdoor run.

1 Read the text above. Which instructions below are for building a chicken coop and which are for playing a game? Write out the words which support your answer.

- a Move the counter across the squares.
- b Add a strong pole for use as a perch.
- c Each player takes it in turns to throw the dice.
- d Use a waterproof material for the roof.
- e Make sure the door is high enough for the person collecting eggs to get in and out easily.

Writing presentation

With your partner decide on a subject you will write instructions for. Write them together. Pick out the key words which show what your instructions are for and write only those down. Read the list to the rest of the class and see if they can give you a heading 'Instructions for …'

2 Choose the correct definition for the words in the box below.

> insulate   roost   protect   ventilate   shelter

- a keep safe from harm
- b to allow fresh air in
- c a safe place
- d a perch birds rest or sleep on
- e prevent the loss of heat

What have I learnt?

Check what you have learnt in this unit.

- I can check my own and other people's writing for clarity.
- I can work out how to spell unusual words.
- I know how important it is that tenses agree in writing.
- I can ask questions to extend my understanding.
- I can write instructions.

Patterns in poetry

Pullin' seine

Splash!	Afternoon tide roll on.
Heave!	Fishermen pullin' seine.
Come on!	Jasmine pulls me along.
Grab!	de nets like we big and strong!
Sink!	our feet deep down in de sands.
Hold!	on tight with both we hands,
Pull!	and tug and pull some more.
Show!	de fish who gonna win this war.
Crash!	We fall and de fish laughin'.
Grunt!	We up and pullin again.
Wet!	and sandy through and through.
Oh no!	I wonder what mama gonna do.
Look!	A big wave rollin' in.
Hurrah!	is now we bound to win!

By Lynn Joseph

> **Glossary**
>
> **seine:** a fishing net that hangs in the water using weights and floats. It can be used from a beach or a boat

I can read and perform poems.

I can comment on writer's choice of language.

Choosing the right words

Talk Partners

Read the poem on page 129 with your partner. Together, practise reading the poem out loud using movement and gestures to show the fishermen's actions. Join up with another pair to show the team effort needed to haul in the nets. Perform this for the class.

1 The table opposite shows words from the poem on page 129. Copy and complete the table with ticks and crosses to show which words are used as imperative verbs. One has been done for you.

Word	Imperative verb
Splash!	
Heave!	✓
Grab!	
Sink!	
Wet!	
Look!	
Hurrah!	
Pull!	

Helpful hints

An **imperative verb** (sometimes called a bossy verb) tells you what to do. For example: *Close* the door.

Using **adverbs** helps to make your writing more interesting for the reader. You can use them to explain how a person speaks, for example: *"Come and help pull in the nets," he urged **loudly**.*

2 Copy and complete the sentences below, adding one of the adverbs in the box to each sentence.

> hurriedly   proudly   tiredly   nervously   urgently   anxiously

a "The tide is coming in, come and help now" they chorused _____.
b "Pull together!" they chanted _____.
c "The fish may get away," they said _____.
d "That's it, we've pulled the nets in!" he panted _____.
e "We will have plenty of fish to sell," they said _____.

Write your own sentence for the adverb you have not used.

Fruits

mangoes
and ripe bananas
jelly coconut
and pomegranates
jack-fruit
and stinking-toe
june plum
and nase-berry

Extract from 'Fruits' by Opal Palmer Adisa

Glossary

jack-fruit: large green fruit from a tropical tree
stinking-toe: a large brown toe-shaped seed pod which is said to smell like feet!
nase-berry: oval brown fruit with sweet red-brown flesh

Talk Partners

Read the short poem extract above with your partner and work out how to perform it to the class. Is it best to separate each line, to read pairs of lines alternately or to read some parts together?

1 Decide on a food type (for example: vegetables, bread or fruit) and make a list of as many varieties as you can. Write a poem in the same style as the extract using your list. Give your poem a title.

Talk Partners

Read your poem to your talk partner. Make changes based on their comments.

2 Write a final, neat version of your poem and illustrate it. Read this out to the rest of the class.

3 Add to your poem using the five senses and an adjective. For example:

mangoes
and ripe bananas *feeling smooth*
jelly coconut
and pomegranates *looking bright*
jack-fruit *tasting sweet*
and stinking-toe *smelling awful*
june plum and
nase-berry *sounding delicious*.

Read these out to the rest of the class.

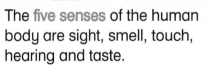

Helpful hints

The five senses of the human body are sight, smell, touch, hearing and taste.

I can interpret imagery.

I can convey ideas about characters in drama.

Performing a poem

This is an extract from a poem about shadows.

Mr Shadow's shoes
Soft-soled shoes
Shush shush
Left and right
Shush shush – out of sight

Mr Shadow's always there
No one knows exactly where
Soft-soled shoes
Silent on the stairs

Shush shush – left and right
Shush shush – out of sight

He's sneaking and he's creeping
He's spying and he's peeping
Soft-soled shoes
Are what he keeps his feet in

Shush shush – left and right
Shush shush – out of sight

By Paul Cookson

Talk Partners

Read the poem above out loud. Think about the subject of the poem – a shadow – and work together to put actions and expression into your reading. Perform this for the class as if one of you is the shadow. Move around the room as you perform it.

1 The writer has used alliteration to make the poem effective. Find five different examples of alliteration in the poem and write them down.

I can convey ideas about characters in drama.

More of the poem

Like a whisper near the door
Ghostly in the corridor
Soft-soled shoes
Slide across the floor

Shush shush – left and right
Shush shush – out of sight
Mr Shadow's shoes
Soft-soled shoes
Soft-soled silent shoes
Soft-soled slippy shoes
Soft-soled slidy shoes
Mr Shadow's soft-soled slippy
slidy shiny silent shoes

Shush shush – left and right
Shush shush – out of sight

He will always find you
Creeping up behind you
He will always find you
Look out … he's behind you

Shush shush – left and right
Shush shush out of sight

Shush shush – left and right
Shush shush – out of sight

Shush shush – left and right
Shush shush – out of sight

Shush shush – left and right
Shush shush – out of sight

Shush shush – left and right
Shush shush – out of sight

By Paul Cookson

Talk Partners Read the rest of the poem with your talk partner.
Work as a pair to perform this poem for your class.
Think about how you will speak and what actions you will use.

Imagery

Sometimes words sound like their meaning. This is called onomatopoeia. Examples of this are *splish* and *splash* which describe water movement. For example: *The rain splashed down.*

1 Put these onomatopoeia words from the cloud into the sentences below.

> whoosh   flutter   chatter   roar   croaking

a   Flags _____ in the wind.
b   The _____ of the lion echoed through the jungle.
c   The pond was alive with the _____ of the frogs.
d   Children _____ happily at the park.
e   We could hear the _____ of the wind.

Try this

Which of the words used in activity 1 are also examples of alliteration?

Helpful hints

Paul Cookson has used simile, alliteration, onomatopoeia and repetition to make this poem effective.

2 Tick the correct column in the table to show the technique shown in these examples from the poem.

	simile	alliteration	onomatopoeia	repetition
Like a whisper near the door				
Shush shush left and right				
Shush shush out of sight				
Mr Shadow's soft-soled slippy slidy shiny silent shoes				
Shush shush				

3 Write a poem using as many of the techniques from Paul Cookson's poem as you can. Keep each line very short, repeat words and phrases and use alliteration.

I can convey ideas about characters in drama.

Talk Partners

Read this poem with your partner. Take it in turns to read a line each as if you were replying to each other. Perform this, with actions, for the rest of the class.

Hurricane

Shut the windows

Bolt the doors
Big rain coming
Climbing up the mountain

Neighbours whisper
Dark clouds gather
Big rain coming
Climbing up the mountain

Gather in the clotheslines
Pull down the blinds
Big wind rising
Coming up the mountain

Branches falling
Raindrops flying
Treetops swaying
People running
Big wind blowing
Hurricane! on the mountain

By Dionne Brand

1 Write words to add alliteration into these sentences.
a The river shimmered as the sun _____.
b The grumpy lion _____ ferociously.
c The match was fast and _____ as both sides were desperate to win.
d The dusty _____ cellar was full of secrets and _____.
e "Stop!" _____ Sanjay as the excited children dashed across the park.

Conversation poems

In this extract two characters are talking to each other, one is old and the other young.

"You are old, Father William," the young man said,
"And your hair has become very white;
And yet you incessantly stand on your head –
Do you think, at your age, it is right?"

"In my youth," Father William replied to his son,
"I feared it might injure the brain;
But, now that I'm perfectly sure I have none,
Why, I do it again and again."

"You are old," said the youth, "as I mentioned before,
And have grown most uncommonly fat;
Yet you turned a back-somersault in at the door –
Pray, what is the reason of that?"

"In my youth," said the sage, as he shook his grey locks,
"I kept all my limbs very supple
By the use of this ointment – one shilling the box –
Allow me to sell you a couple?"

From Alice's Adventures In Wonderland *by Lewis Carroll*

1 Read the poem above. The two characters are referred to in different ways in this poem. Copy and complete the table to show which character each description refers to?

	The old man	The young man
the youth		
the sage		
Father William		
his son		

Talk Partners

Why can Lewis Carroll not use many pronouns to refer to the two characters in this poem? Discuss with your talk partner why this would have been confusing for the reader.

Helpful hints

Sometimes two different letters make the same sound. In some words **oi** and **oy** sound the same. For example **oil** and **joy**. We use **oy** in the middle or at the end of words and **oi** at the beginning or in the middle.

2 Copy and complete these sentences. Put the right letters into the words.
  a   The little girl played with her t_____.
  b   The sandwich was wrapped in f_____l to keep it m____st.
  c   Mum rubbed _____ntment into the graze.
  d   The little b____ has some new shoes.

Questions

"You are old," said the youth, "one would hardly suppose
That your eye was as steady as ever;
Yet you balanced an eel on the end of your nose –
What made you so awfully clever?"

"I have answered three questions, and that is enough,"
Said his father; "don't give yourself airs!
Do you think I can listen all day to such stuff?
Be off, or I'll kick you down stairs!"

From Alice's Adventures In Wonderland *by Lewis Carroll*

Talk Partners

Read the next verses of the poem above. Father William says "I have answered three questions, and that is enough". Talk about the questions the young man has asked and think of another question.

Glossary

give yourself airs: to act better than you are.

1 With your talk partner write two more verses using the same style as Lewis Carroll. Perform these for the rest of the class, each taking the role of one of the characters. Use actions and perform in character.

2 The poet has used an idiom *don't give yourself airs* where the words used do not mean what they actually say. Match the idioms in the box to their meanings.
   a   Read between the lines
   b   Have a change of heart
   c   Second to none
   d   Play it by ear
   e   Call it a day

   the best   alter a decision
   to find the hidden meaning in something
   stop doing something
   deal with things as they happen

3 Copy and complete the table with ticks to show which styles and themes are used in these two poems.

Style and theme	Father William	Mr Shadow's shoes
conversation		
alliteration		
simile		
movement in performance		
an air of mystery		

Writing a poem

Once when Gervase Phinn visited a school he was met by a girl who loved poetry.
He wrote down the conversation they had.

'I'm very good at poetry you know.'
'Would you like to see my poems?' she continued.
'I would love to,' I replied.
'Do you write poetry?' Helen asked, handing me a copy of her poem.
'Yes, I do,' I replied.
'Do you get the rhythms?'
'Yes.'
'And the rhymes?'
'Sometimes'.
'Do you illustrate your poems?'
'No, I'm afraid I don't.'
She smiled. 'I do,' she said. 'I think it makes them
look nicer on the page.'
'And why are you so good at writing poetry?'
I asked.
She sighed. 'Oh, I don't really know. I like to read them.
We have lots of poetry books in our classroom and our teacher
reads us a poem every day.'

By Gervase Phinn

Talk Partners

Read the dialogue above. With a partner, work out how to turn
this conversation into a poem. Remember to give each of the
characters their own verse. Think about using words that rhyme
and any other techniques you have learnt about (alliteration,
simile, repetition and so on).

Perhaps you could start like this:

> I'm very good at poetry, it makes things sound so great
> I'm very good at poems although I'm only eight.
> I'm very good at poems, I like to write them out
> Poetry and poems is what I'm all about!

When you have finished perform your poem for the class.
Remember to use actions and expression to show each character.

Talking and replying

This is an extract from the poem *Mum'll be coming home today.*

Mum'll be coming home today.
It's three weeks she's been away.
When Dad's alone
All we eat is cold meat
Which I don't like and he burns the toast
I want just brown
And I hate taking the ash-can down.

And can we have grilled tomatoes
Spanish onions and roast potatoes
And will you sing me
'I'll never more roam' when I'm in bed
When you've come home?

Mum's reply
If you like your toast done just brown
Then take it out before it burns.
So you hate taking the ash-can down?
Well …

By Michael Rosen

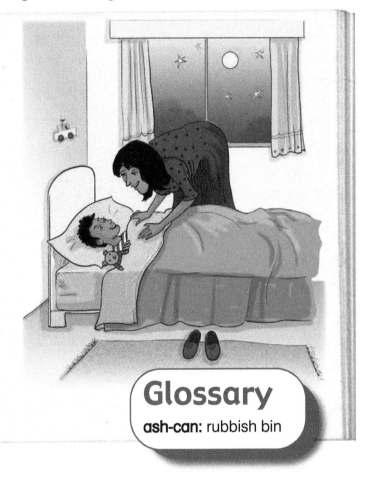

Glossary

ash-can: rubbish bin

Talk Partners

Read the poem together and talk about the rest of Mum's *reply*. Think about the points she needs to reply to: the ash-can; the meal; singing the song to the child in bed.

1. Write the last verse of the poem above using the ideas you discussed with your talk partner. Read your new verses to your talk partner. Make suggestions to improve each other's work.

2. Redraft your verse, making any improvements which you discussed with your talk partner.

3. Practise performing the poem. Remember to add gestures and to act like the character's part you are reading. Perform this for the rest of the class.

Dad's story

Talk Partners

You have written Mum's reply in activity 1 on page 139. Now talk about how Dad would join in this conversation. Think about the things that both Mum and the child have already said. How would Dad reply and would he want to add anything new?

1 Turn some of the words in the poem on page 139 into dialogue. Copy and complete the table.

Word in the poem	Dialogue
All we eat is cold meat which I don't like.	"Dad, I don't like eating cold meat."
And I hate taking the ash-can down.	
So you hate taking the ash-can down.	
He burns the toast, I want just brown.	

Writing presentation

Using the same patterns and ideas from the first verse of the poem, write Dad's verse. Try to show how he feels when Mum is not home.

Talk Partners

Share your new verses. Read them aloud to your partner using gestures and actions. Suggest how your partner's work can be improved. Together, redraft and write out your final version. Put the whole poem together. Ask a third person to join you to read the first verse – you and your partner each read Mum and Dad's verses. Use actions and gestures.

What have I learnt?

Check what you have learnt in this unit:
* I know how to use gestures, actions and speech in drama.
* I know how imagery is created in poetry using techniques like repetition, similes and alliteration.
* I can plan and write a poem.
* I can evaluate my own and others' writing.

PRACTICE TEST 3

Non-fiction

Read the text and answer ALL the questions that follow.

How to build a wildlife pond

First choose the sunniest site in your garden that you can. Make sure that you place your pond near a water supply so you can keep the water topped up.

Mark out the shape of your pond with a hosepipe or some rope. Your finished pond will look smaller than the shape you make.

Then get digging!

Dig out the whole area straight down about 30 cm. (Use this earth to make a new flowerbed somewhere else in the garden.)

Your next job is to dig a deep hole in the middle, while leaving about 60 cm of earth undisturbed all the way round.

Now fit the liner.

This is best done on a day with no wind! Get as many friends to help as you can. Open out the liner and drape it over the pond so that there is plenty to spare all the way round.

Next add water. Once the pond is full, carefully cut off any extra liner at water level leaving about 30 cm all the way around.

You've finished. Welcome to your new wildlife pond!

1   Find and copy a 'handy hint' from this set of instructions.   (1)

2   Where could the following 'handy hint' fit into the instructions: (1)
    'Use a sharp knife but be careful'?

3   Why is it important to have a water supply near the pond?   (1)

4   Find three words which tell you that these instructions are in sequence.   (1)

5   Find and write three imperative verbs.   (3)

6   Why does the writer add an exclamation mark after 'Then get digging!'   (1)
    Choose one of these options:
    a   To show you have nearly finished.
    b   To show it will be hard work.
    c   To show surprise.
    d   To show it will be done quickly.

7   Write out the contraction in this sentence in full: You've finished.   (1)

8   These instructions do not include a list of 'what you need'. Write out that list.   (3)

9   Explain why the writer says that it is best to fit the liner on a day with no wind.   (1)

10 What other new garden feature does the writer say you can make?   (1)

11 Write a more interesting title for these instructions.   (1)

12 The writer has used a superlative: 'sunniest'.   (3)
    Write the superlative for these words:
    a   healthy
    b   busy
    c   empty
    d   quiet
    e   tired

13 Answer this question using correctly punctuated direct speech: (1)
    "Where is the best place in the garden for a wildlife pond?"

14 Think about something that you take care of. This might be a plant, a pet or   (4)
    something you have to clean. Write the instructions for someone else to do
    this. Remember to include a title which tells them what the task is. Tell them
    what to do step-by-step and include all the equipment they will need.

Fiction

Read the poem and answer ALL the questions which follow.

Parents' Evening

So you are Matthew's mother
Then you must be his dad?
I'm so very pleased to meet you,
I am extremely glad.
He's such a gifted pupil,
And such a little dear,
There's been a vast improvement
In all his work this year.
His writing is exceptional,
So beautifully neat,
His spelling quite incredible,
His poetry a treat.
His number work is flawless
And his painting so inspired.
He's interested and lively,
And he's never ever tired.
He's amazingly athletic,
And excels in every sport.
Your Matty is the brightest child
That I have ever taught.
I should say he's gifted – he comes top in every test.
In fact in every single subject
Your Matthew is the best!
I must say Mr and Mrs Flynn,
You're fortunate to have a child like him.

By Gervase Phinn

1   Matthew is described as an exceptional learner. Find three synonyms for the   (3)
    word 'exceptional' in the poem.

2   The teacher says; 'I am extremely glad'. What word class is 'extremely'?   (1)

3 Punctuate these sentences correctly. (3)
   a Matthew is a gifted learner the teacher said
   b We are very pleased with his work they answered
   c Well done Matthew Mum and Dad said
   d Can we see some examples of his writing please they asked
   e Of course said the teacher I will fetch them now

4 Explain why there is an apostrophe in the word 'you're'. (1)

5 Put a prefix from this list in front of the underlined words in these sentences. (3)

> re-   mis-   im-   un-   ir-

   a It was <u>possible</u> to believe the teacher. **b** We have to <u>build</u> the shed this weekend.
   c The story is <u>believable</u>.   **d** The children <u>behaved</u> at school.
   e The clock's tick was <u>regular</u>.

6 Write a comparative for each of these words. (3)
   a heavy   **b** strange
   c dry   **d** rich
   e angry

7 Underline the homophones in this sentence and explain the difference (1)
between the two words.

They bought a new sail for the boat in the sale.

8 Change the underlined words in these sentences into pronouns. (1)

The teacher told Matthew's parents that <u>Matthew</u> was an excellent sport.
<u>Matthew's parents</u> were delighted.

9 The writer has not used similes to describe Matthew. Change each of these lines (3)
so that it includes a simile. The first one has been done for you.
   a So beautifully neat. As neat as a new pin.
   b He's interested and lively. As lively as _____.
   c He's amazingly athletic. As athletic as _____.
   d Your Matty is the brightest child. As bright as _____.
   e You're fortunate to have a child like him. As lucky as _____.

10 You have been told that a new learner is joining your class next week. (4)
Write a letter which welcomes this child to the school and gives some helpful
advice. For example: *Remember to bring your jumper, it is cold in the hall.*